GRAFFITI COLORING BOOK
FOR ADULTS

A COLLECTION OF
GRAFFITI PIECES AND
BLACK BOOK SKETCHES
BY ARTIST SAMUEL NYGARD

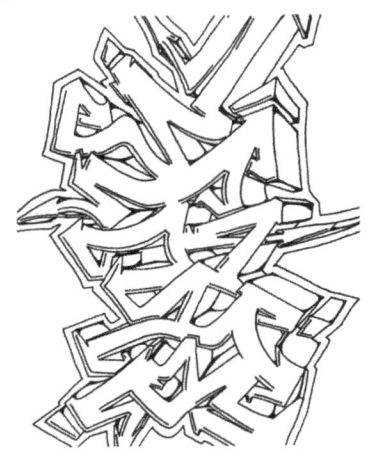

PHUK

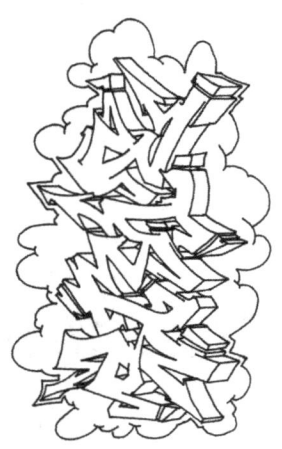

STYLE

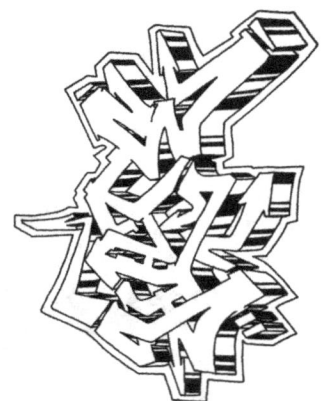

HATE

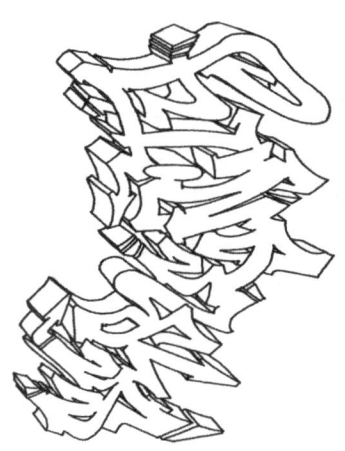

SERENITY

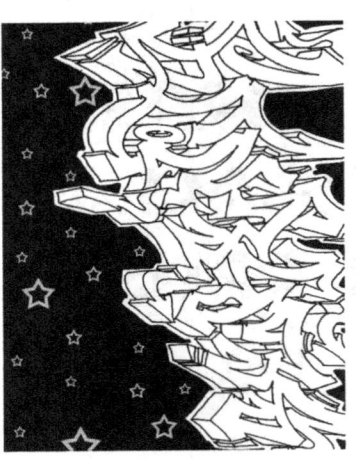

SERENITY

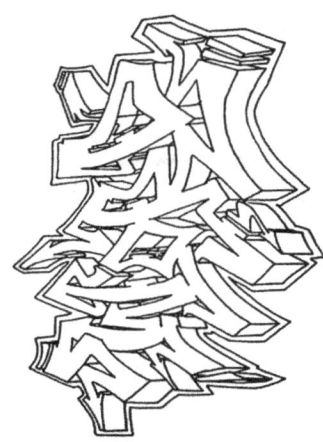

WORD

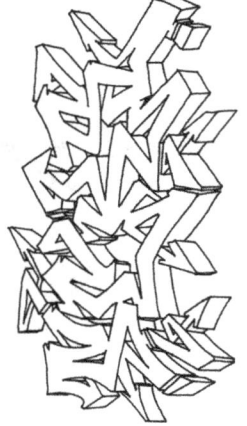

SEKS

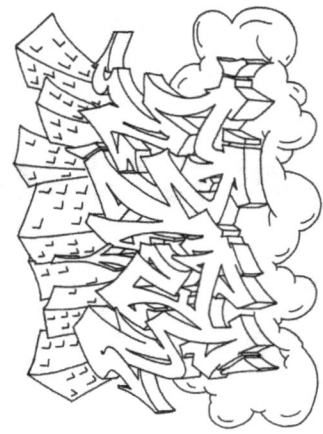

SEKS

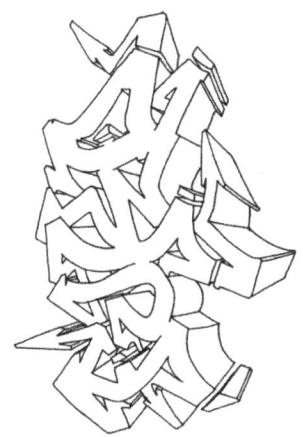

FUKD

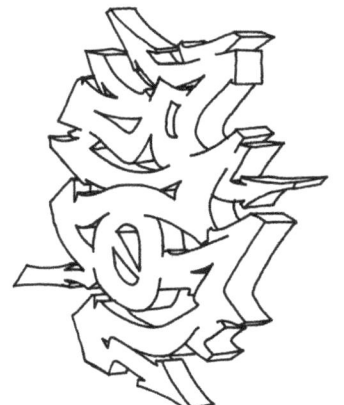

LOVE

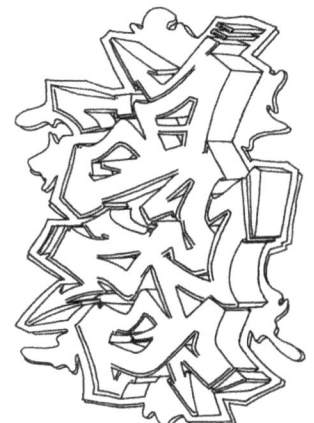

REB

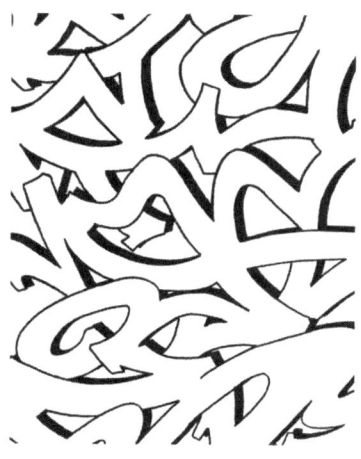

SIRE

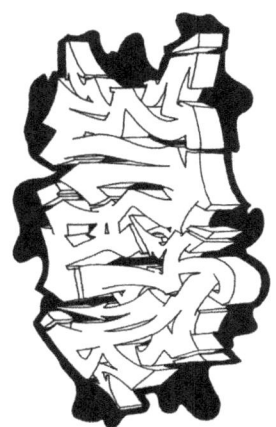

SLAVE

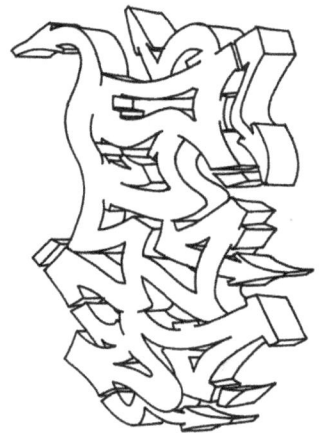

SYCO

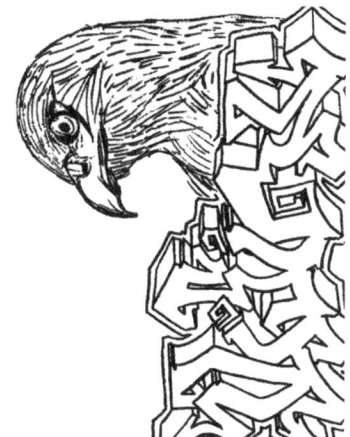

VISION

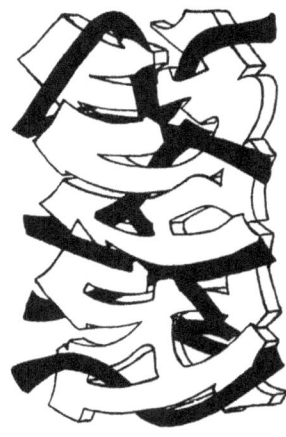

WAR/PEACE

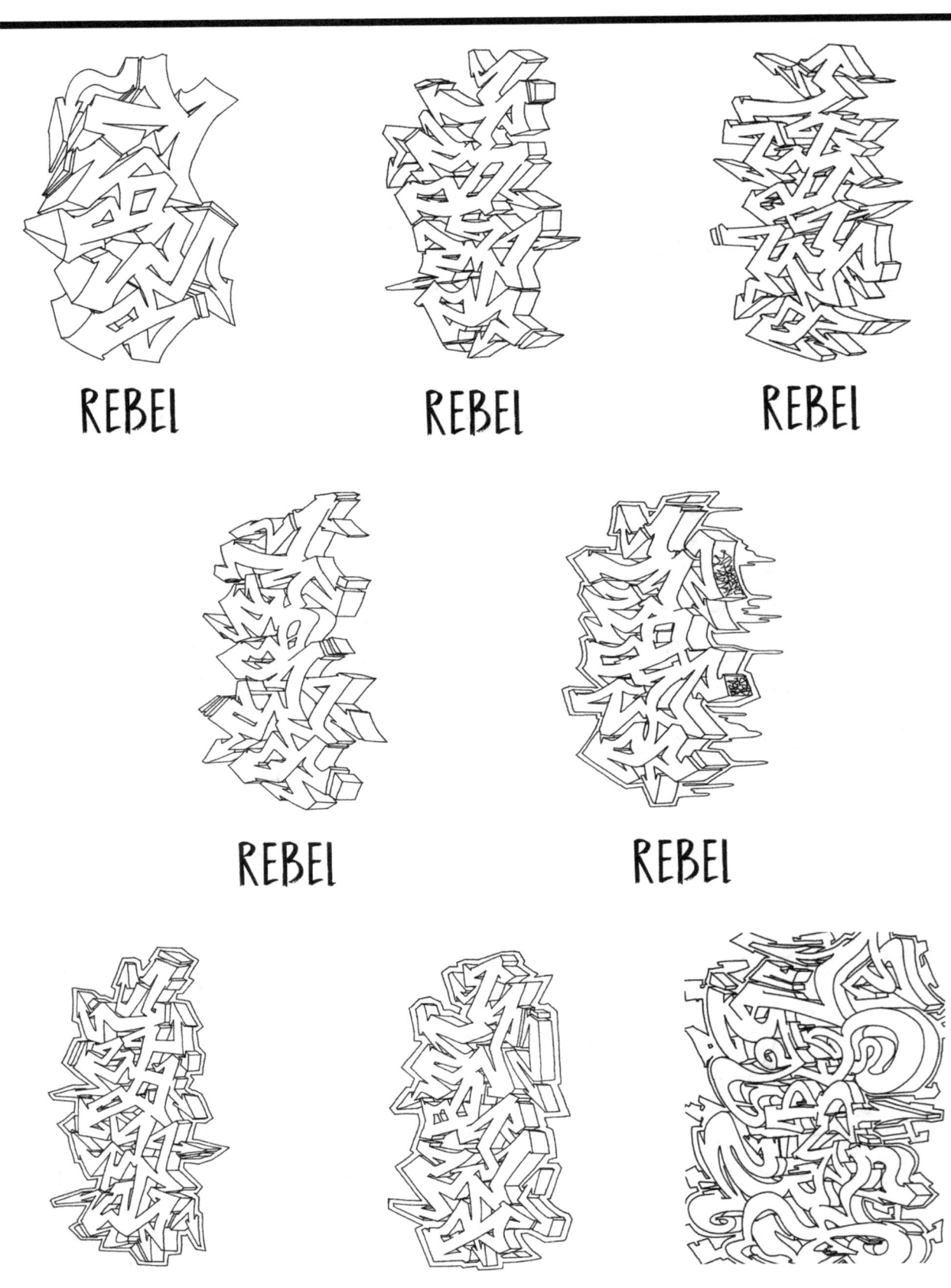

REBEL

REBEL

REBEL

REBEL

REBEL

REBEL

REBEL

REBEL

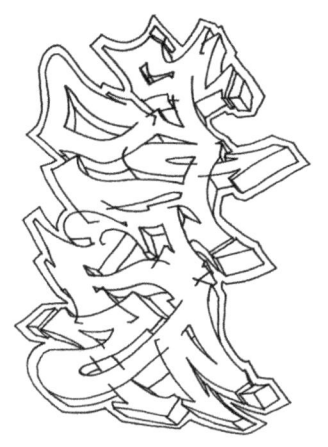

STYLE

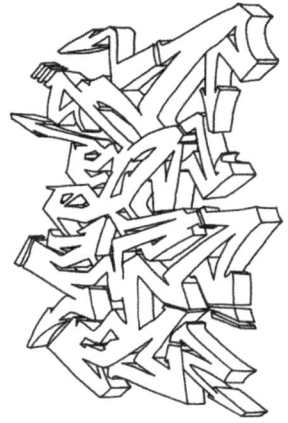

REBEL

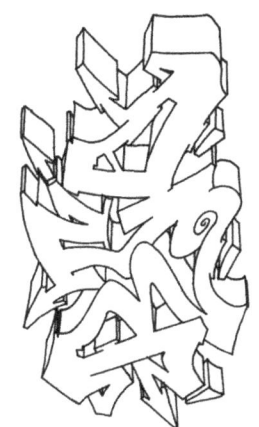

RCD

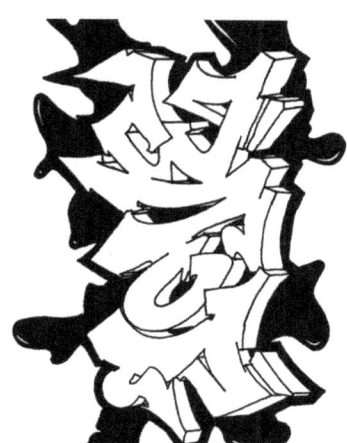

LOVE

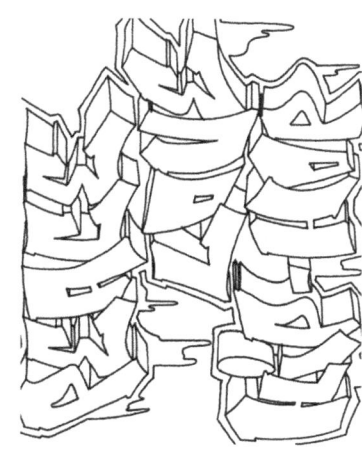

PEACE LOVE HIP-HOP

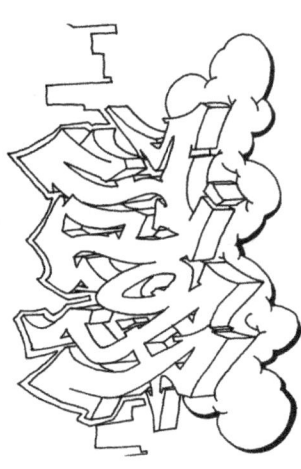

HOPE

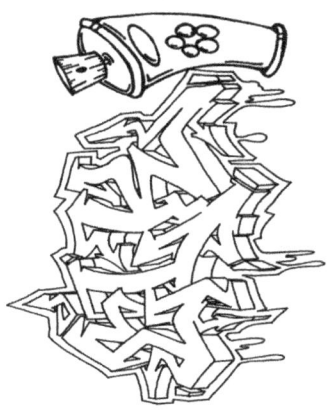

GLK

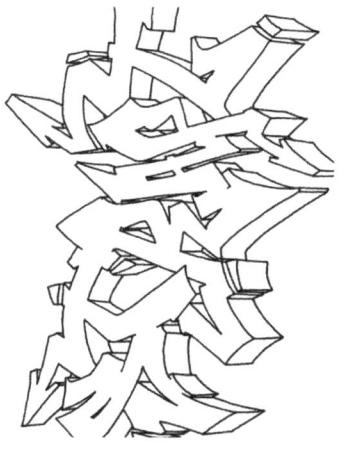

STRAPT

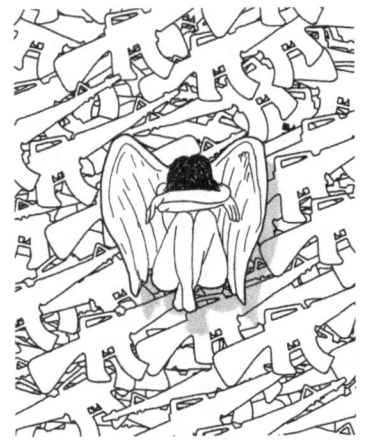

ANGEL N GUNZ

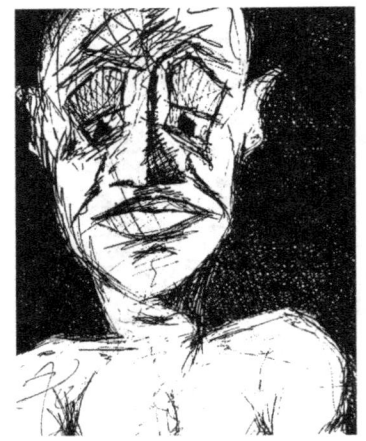

LOST SOUL

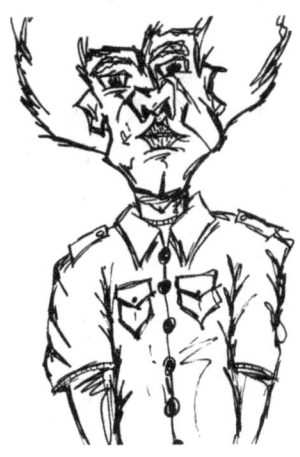

MANIAC

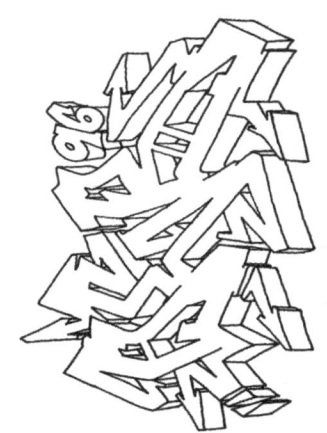

DEB 96

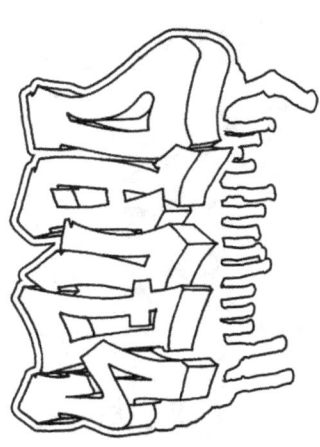

SQUAD

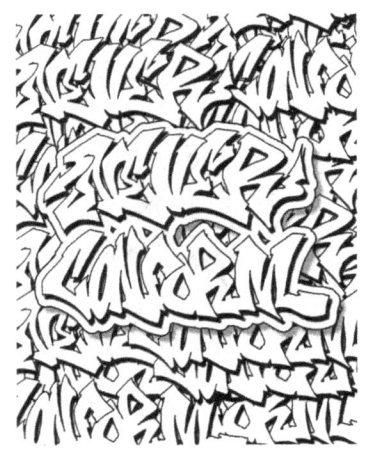

NEVER CONFORM

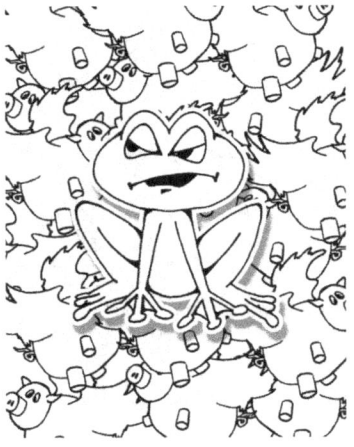

FROG N PIGS

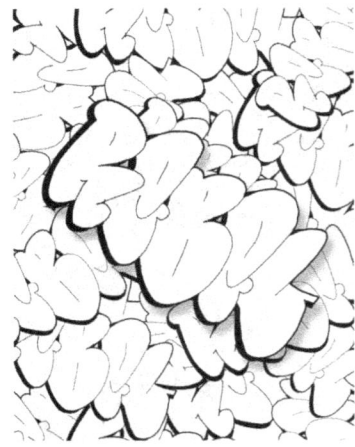

REBEL

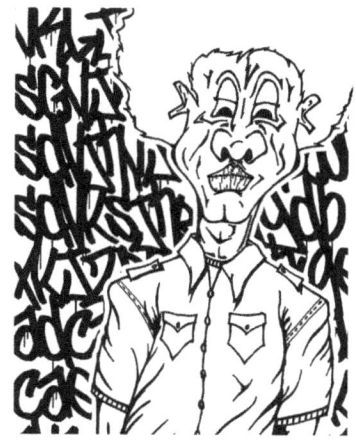

TAG MAN

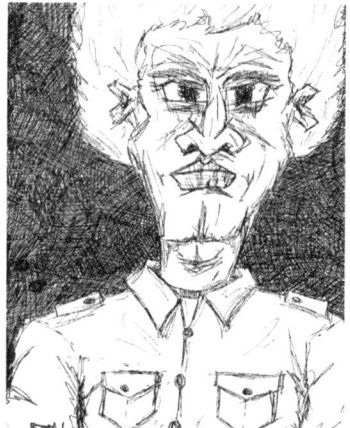

KILLA

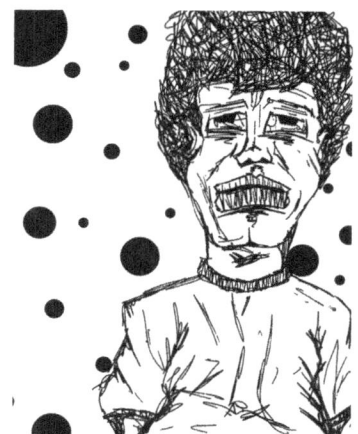

FISH MAN

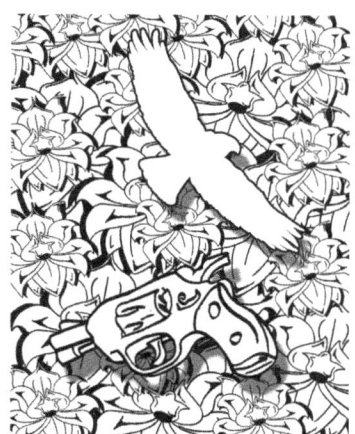

SHOOT HIGH

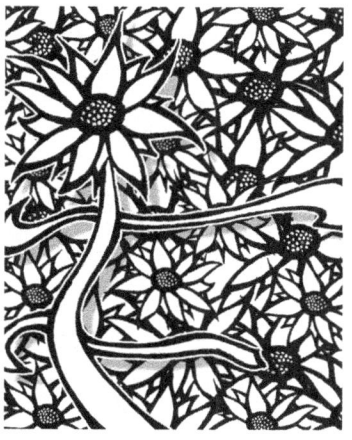

FLOWERS

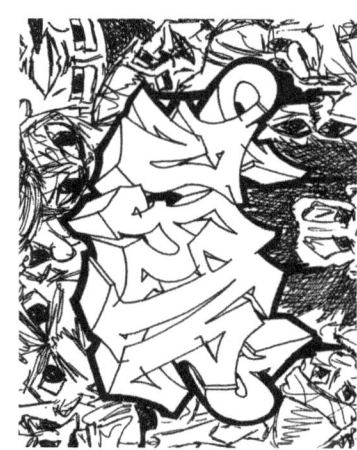

NYC

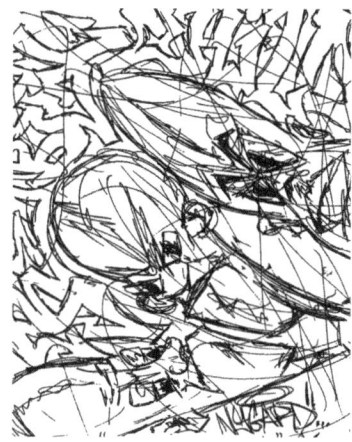

REBEL CHILD

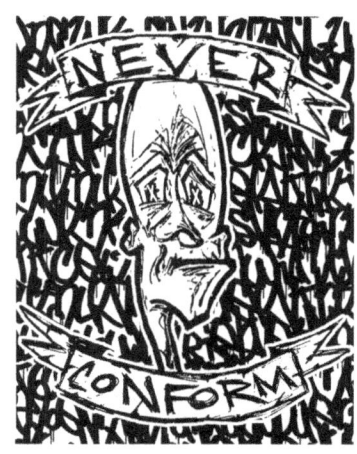

NEVER CONFORM

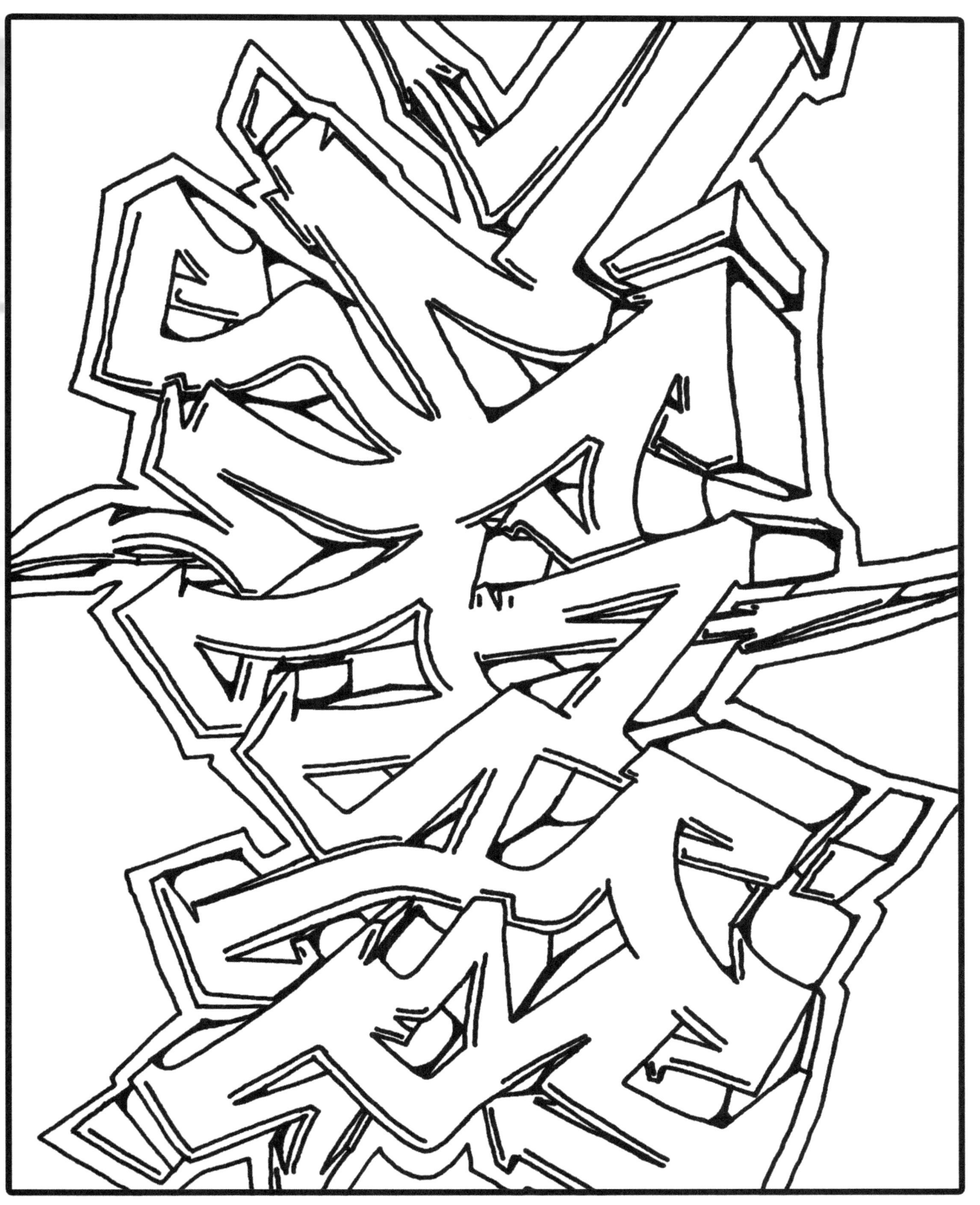

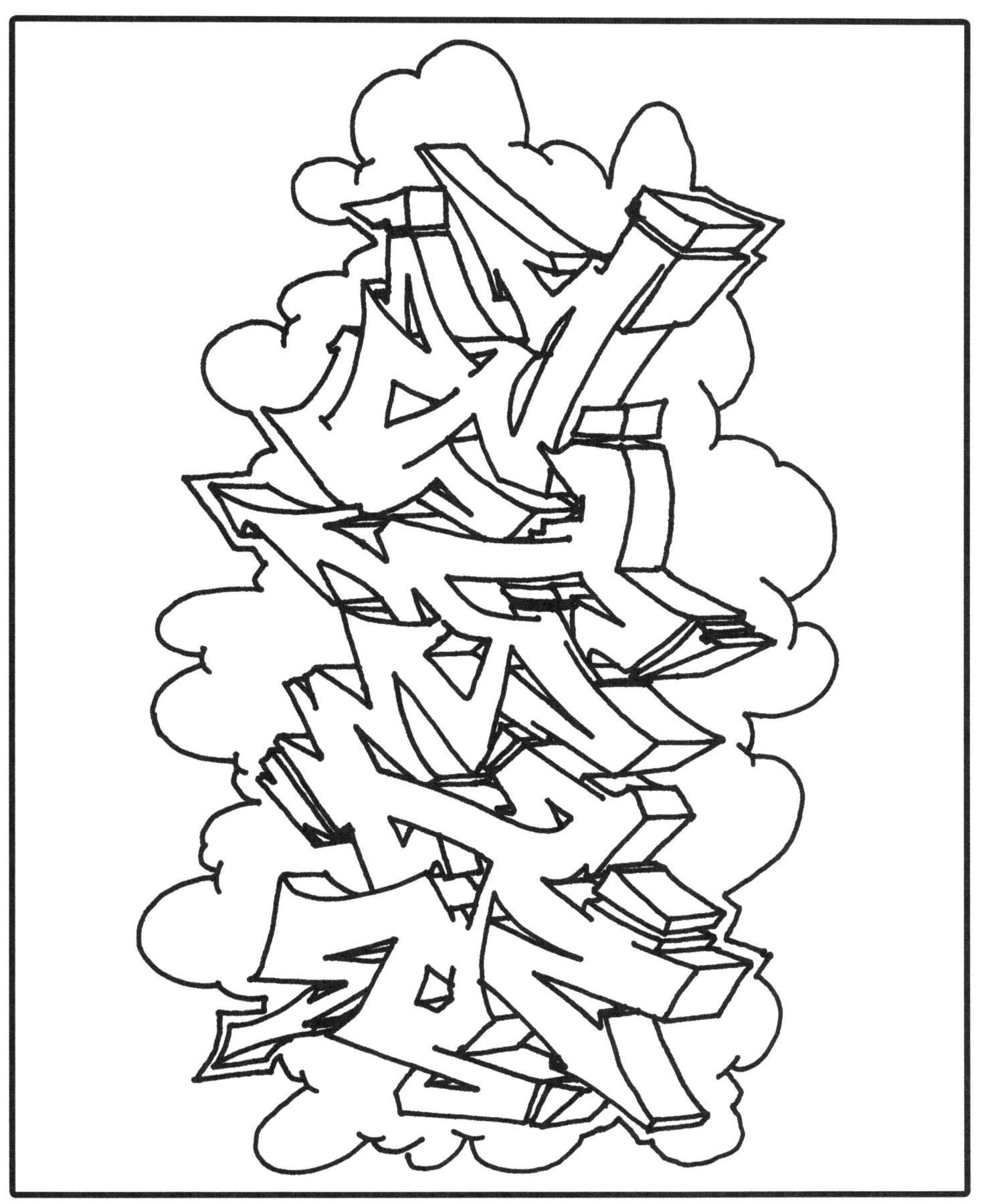

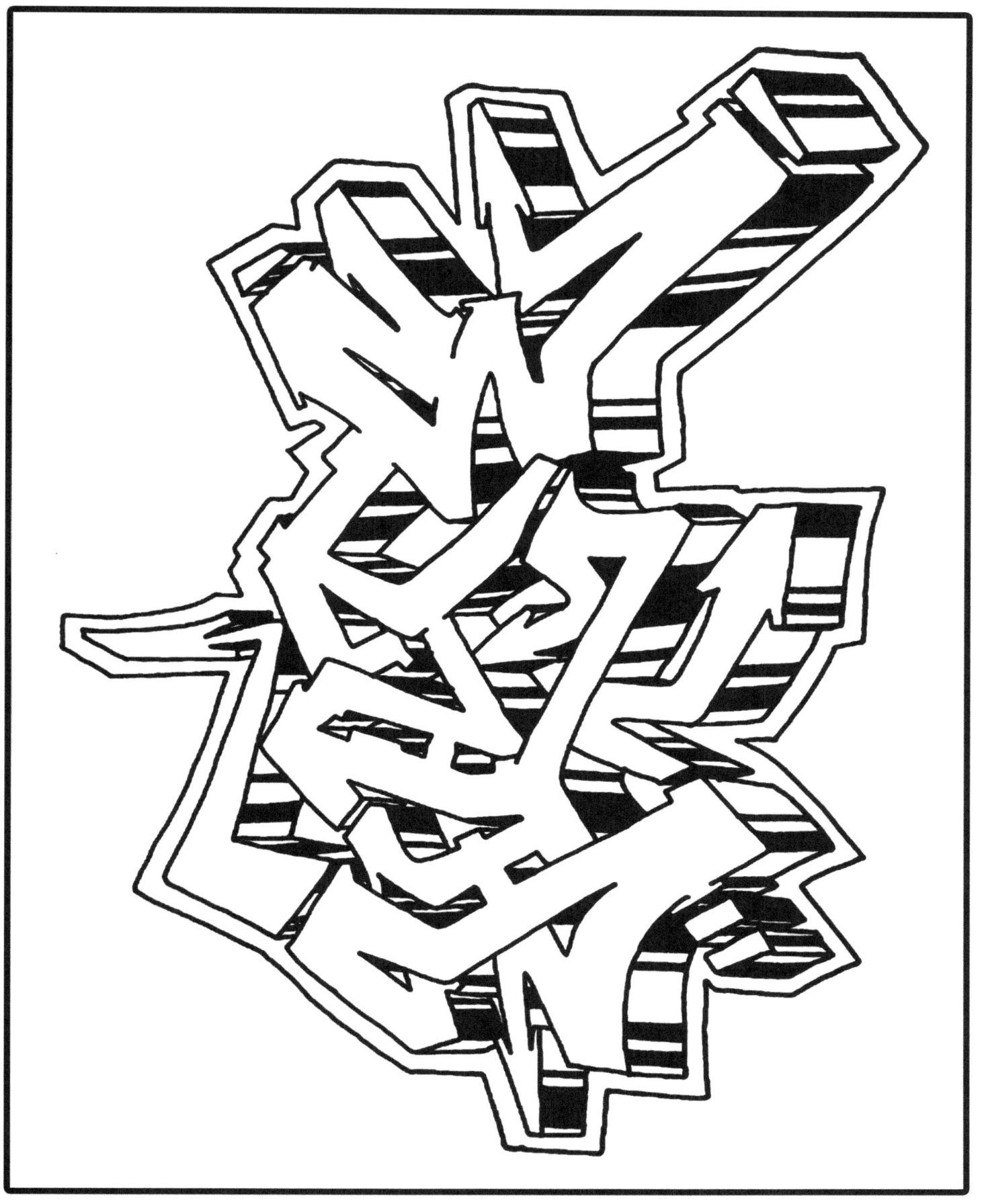

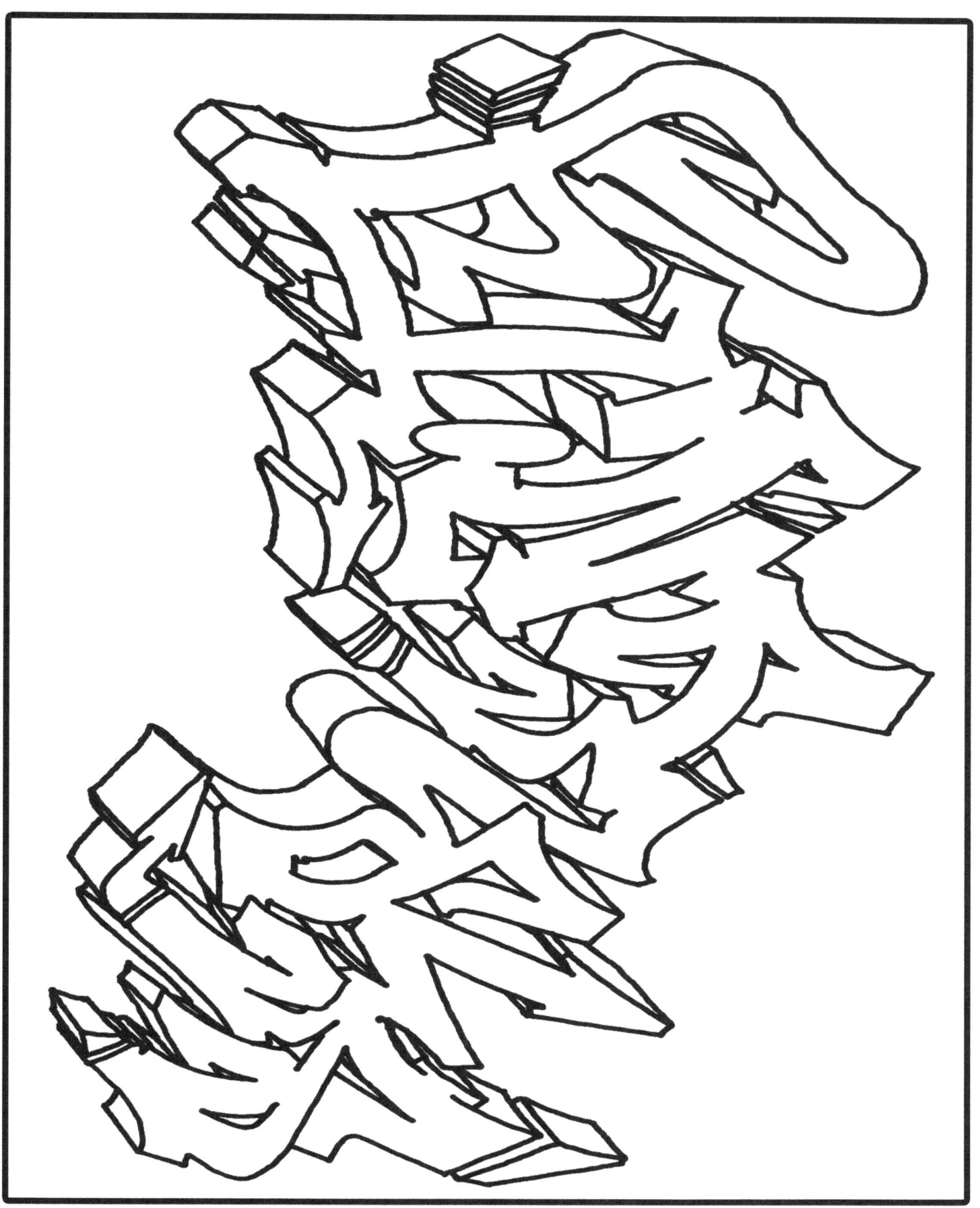

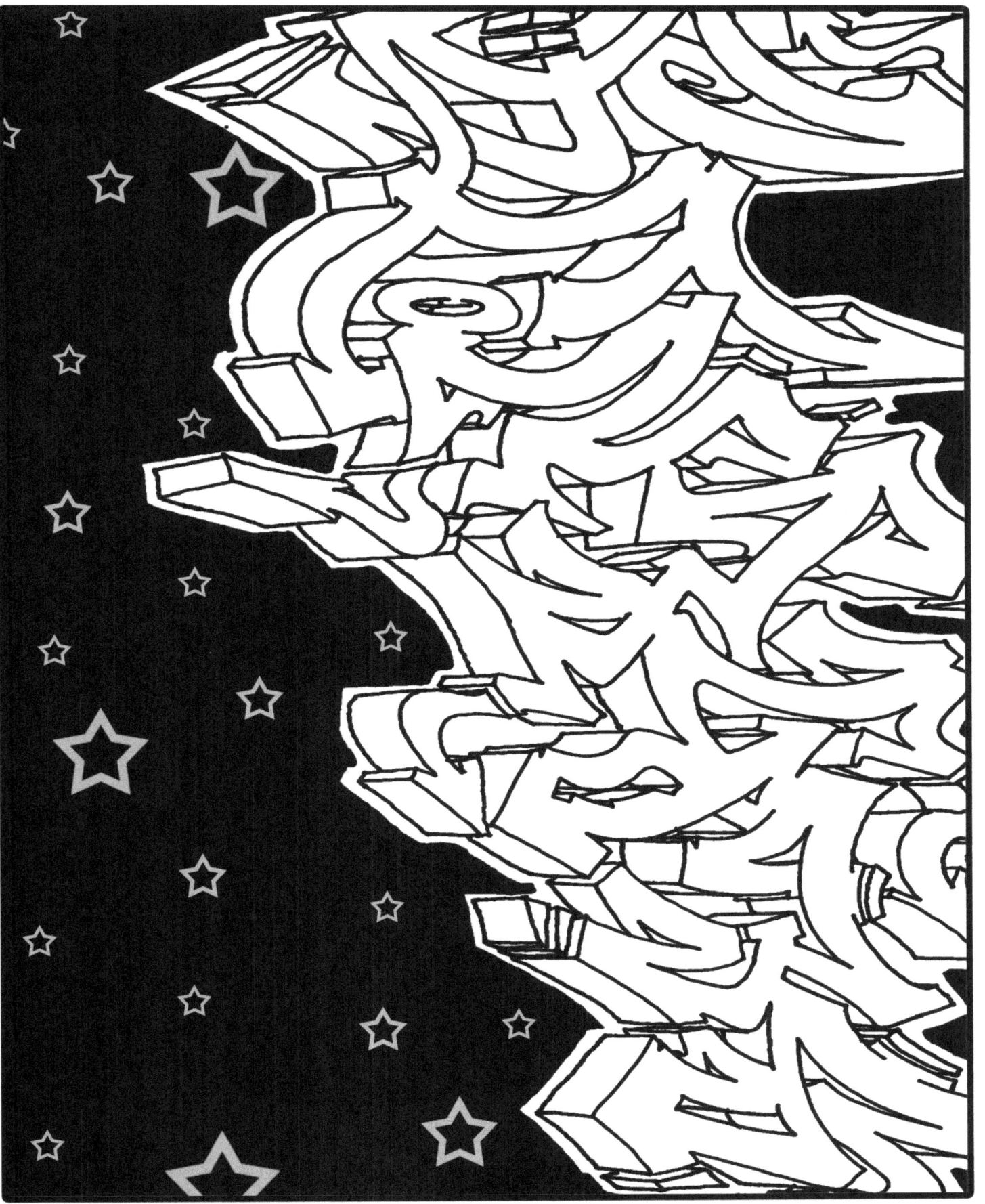

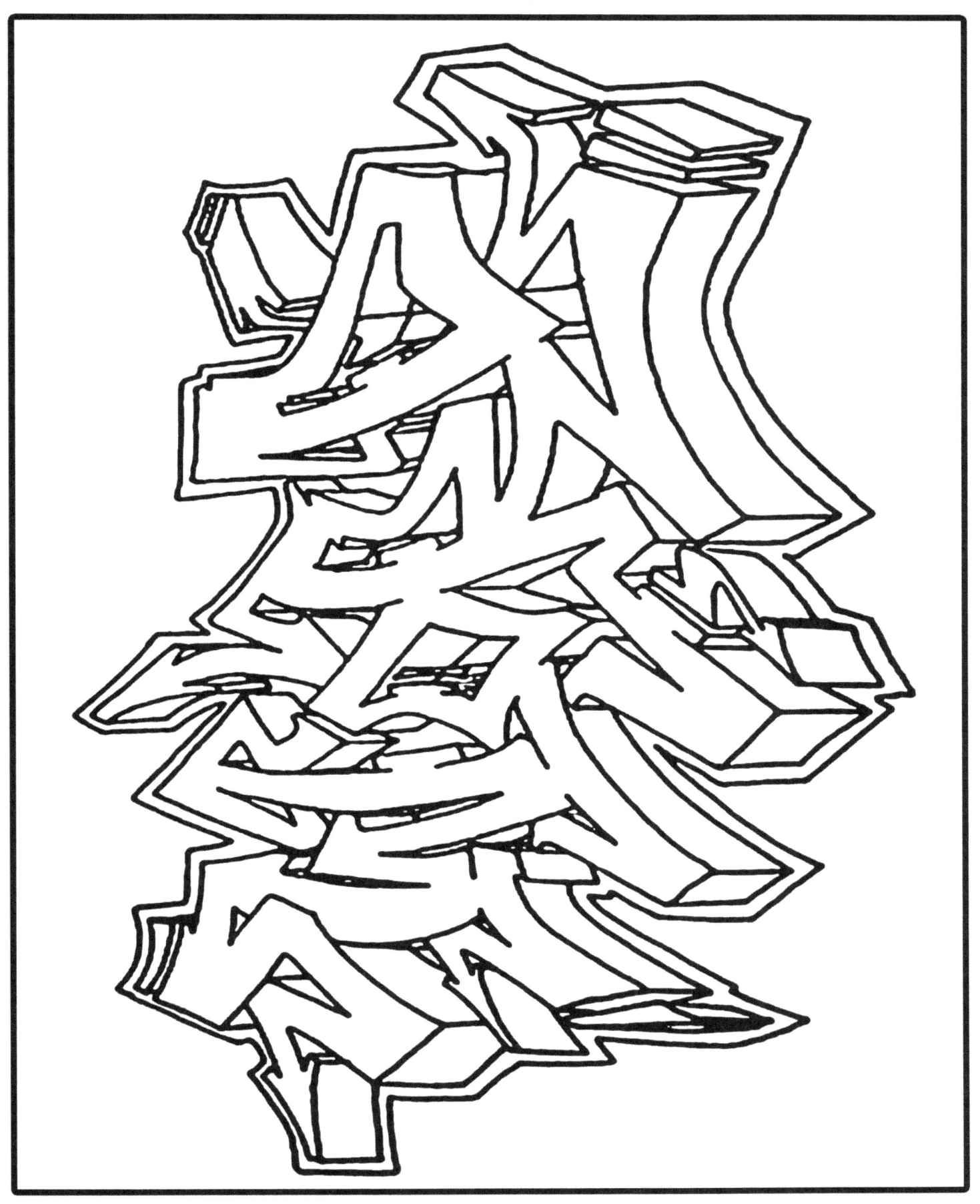

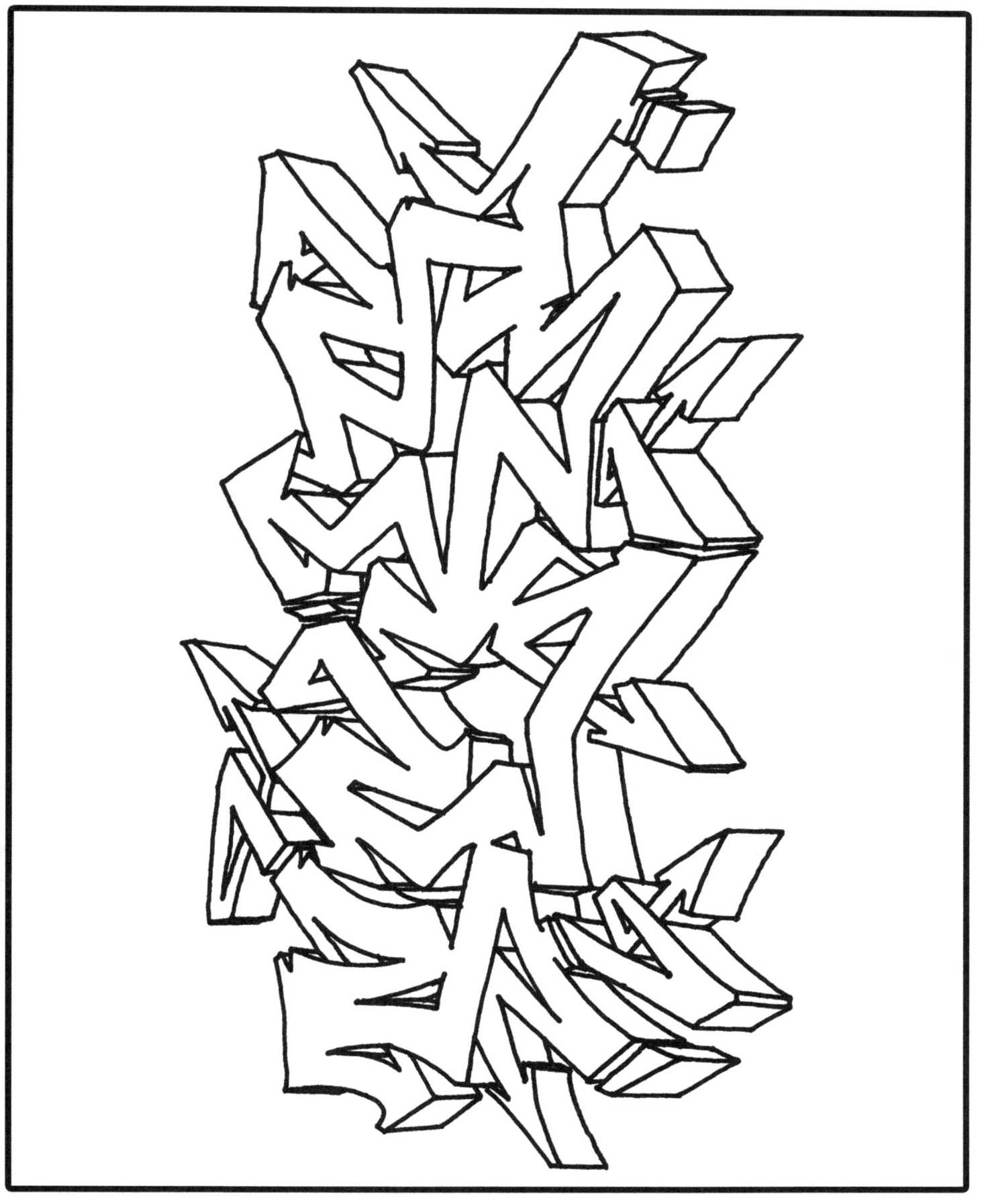

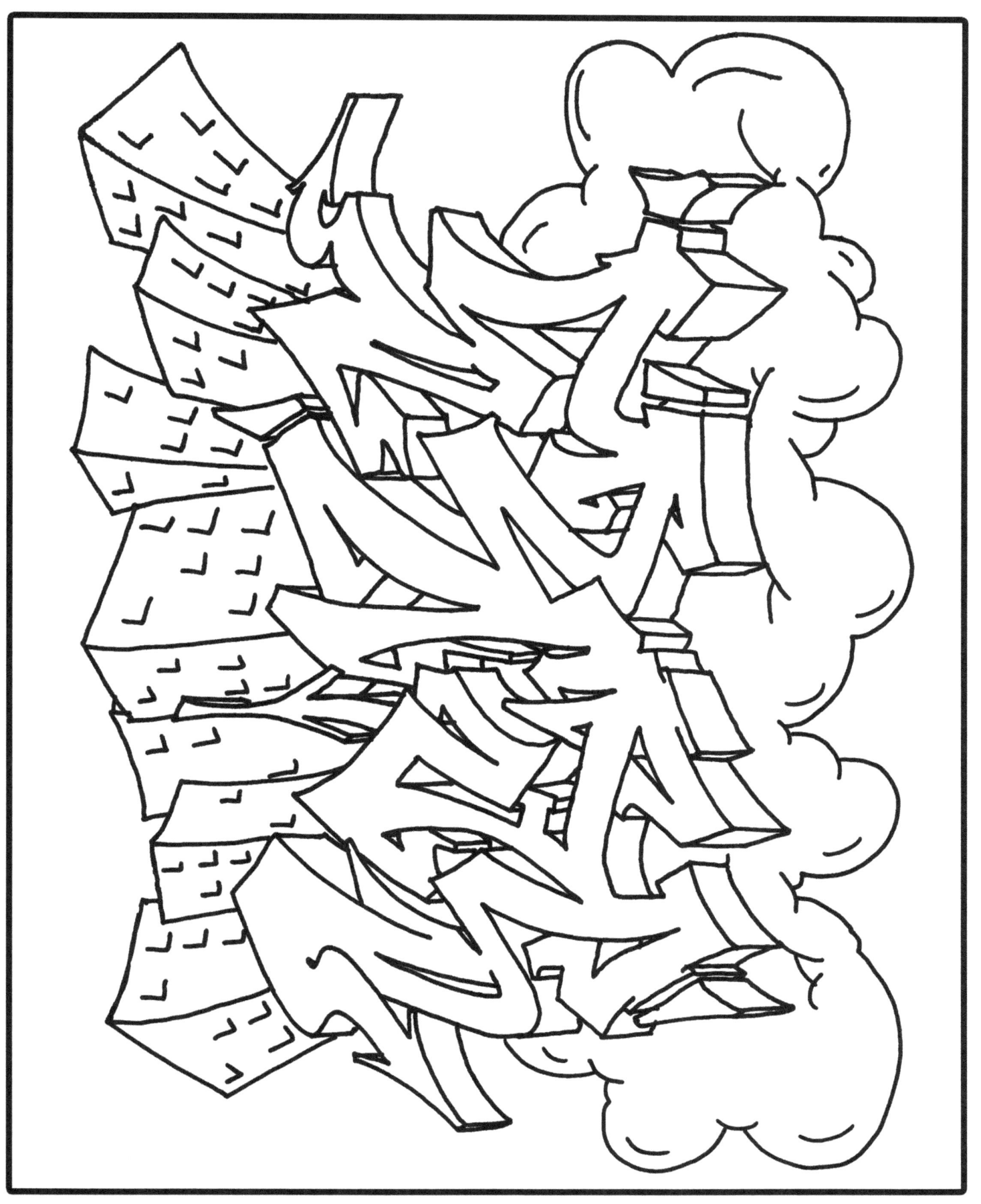

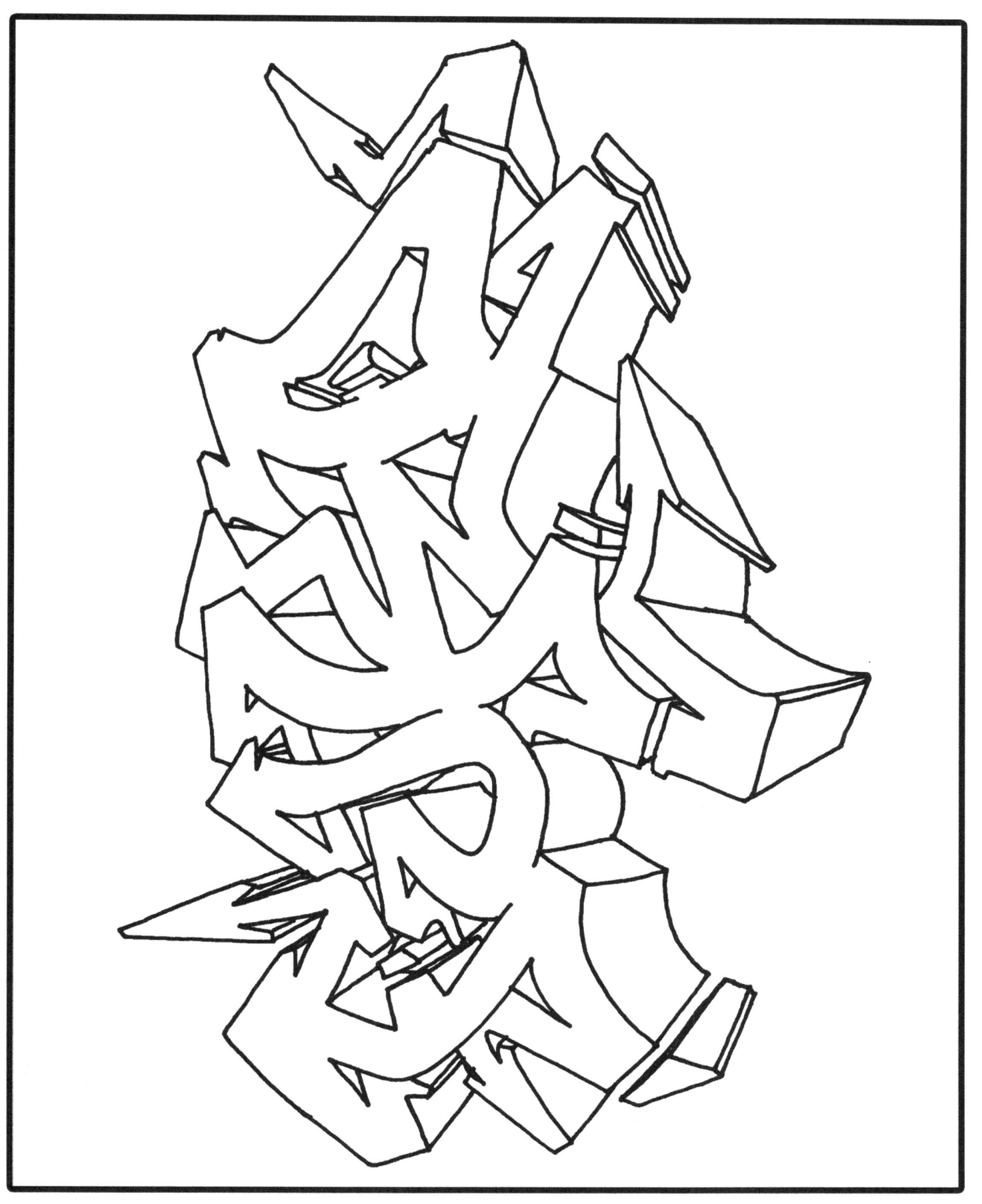

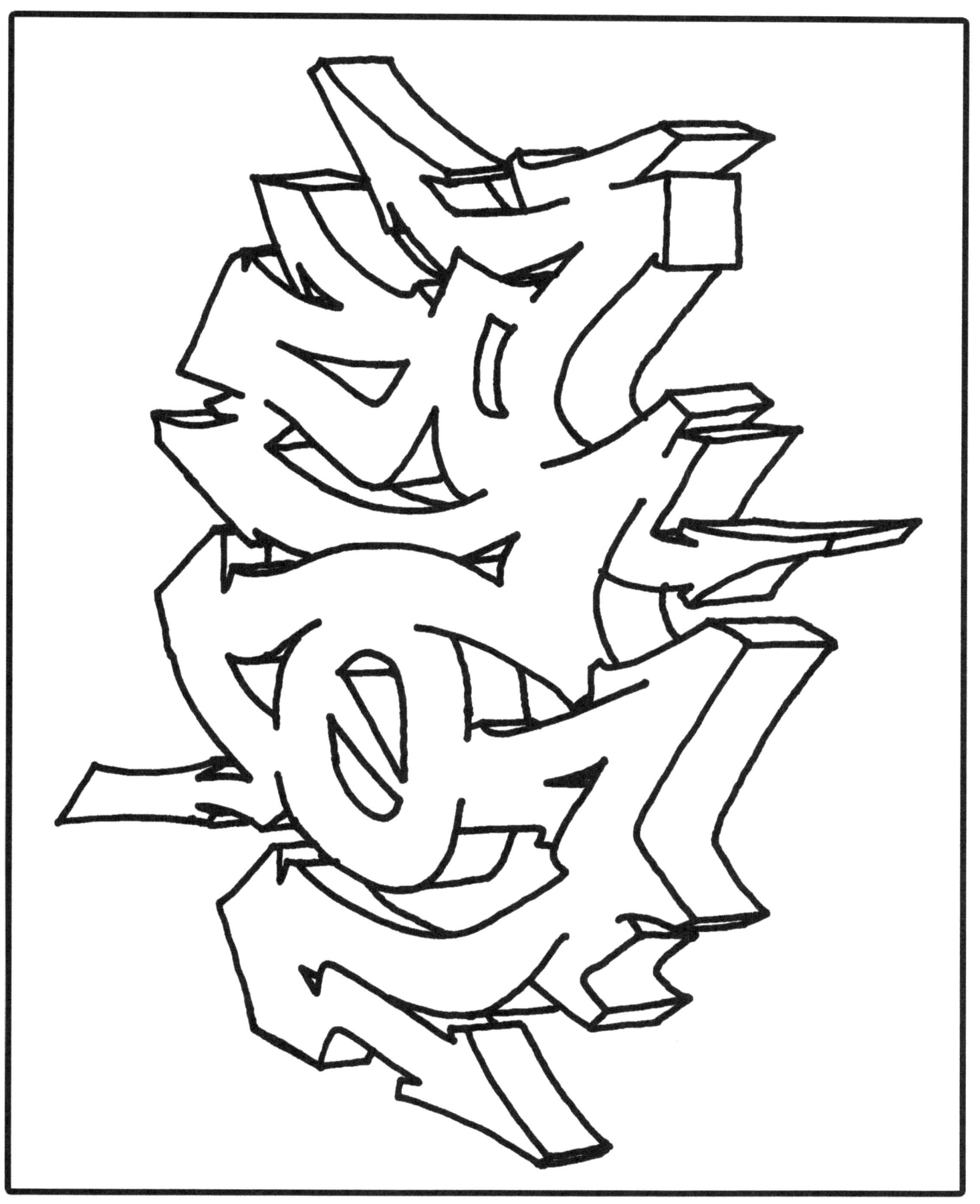

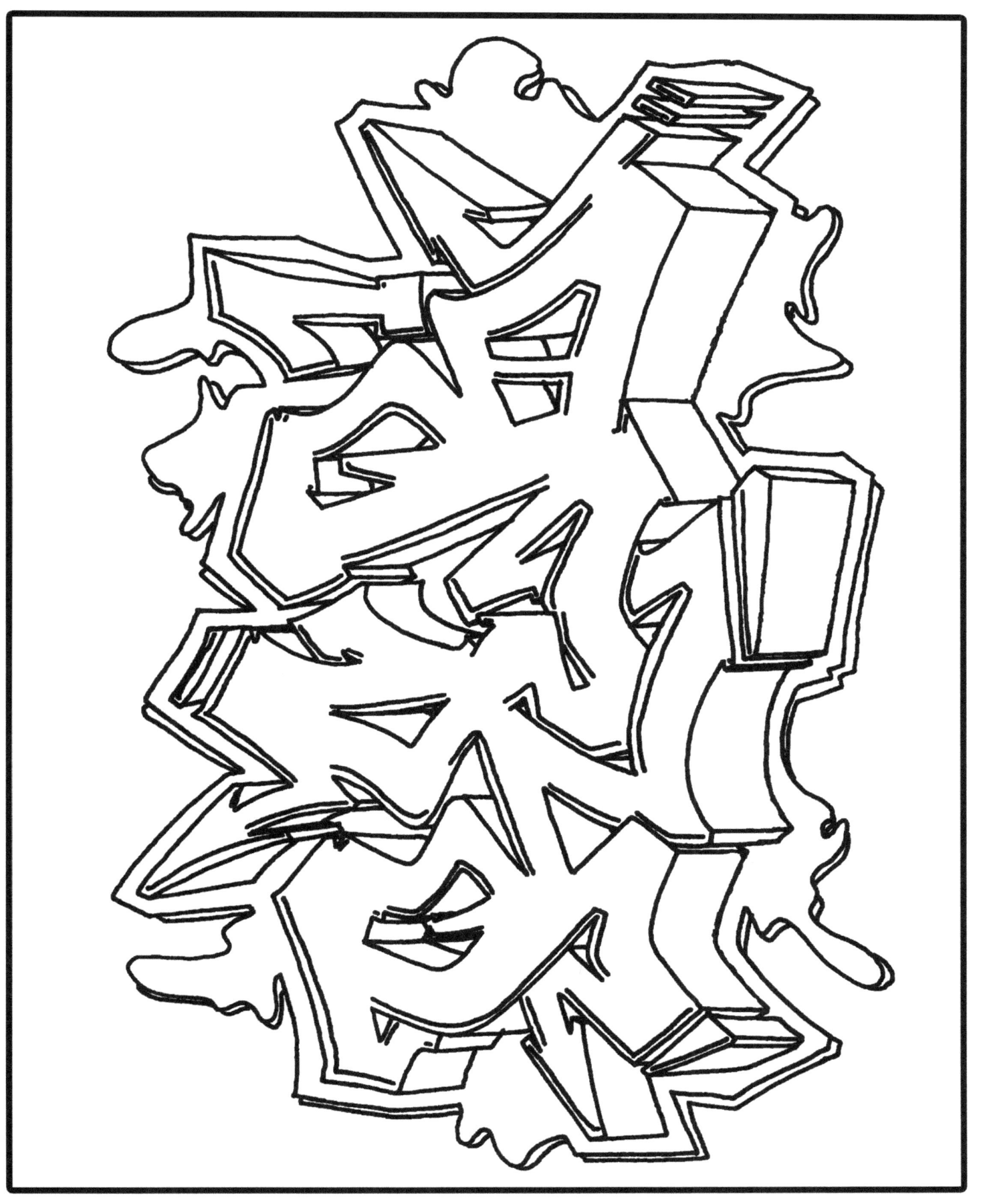

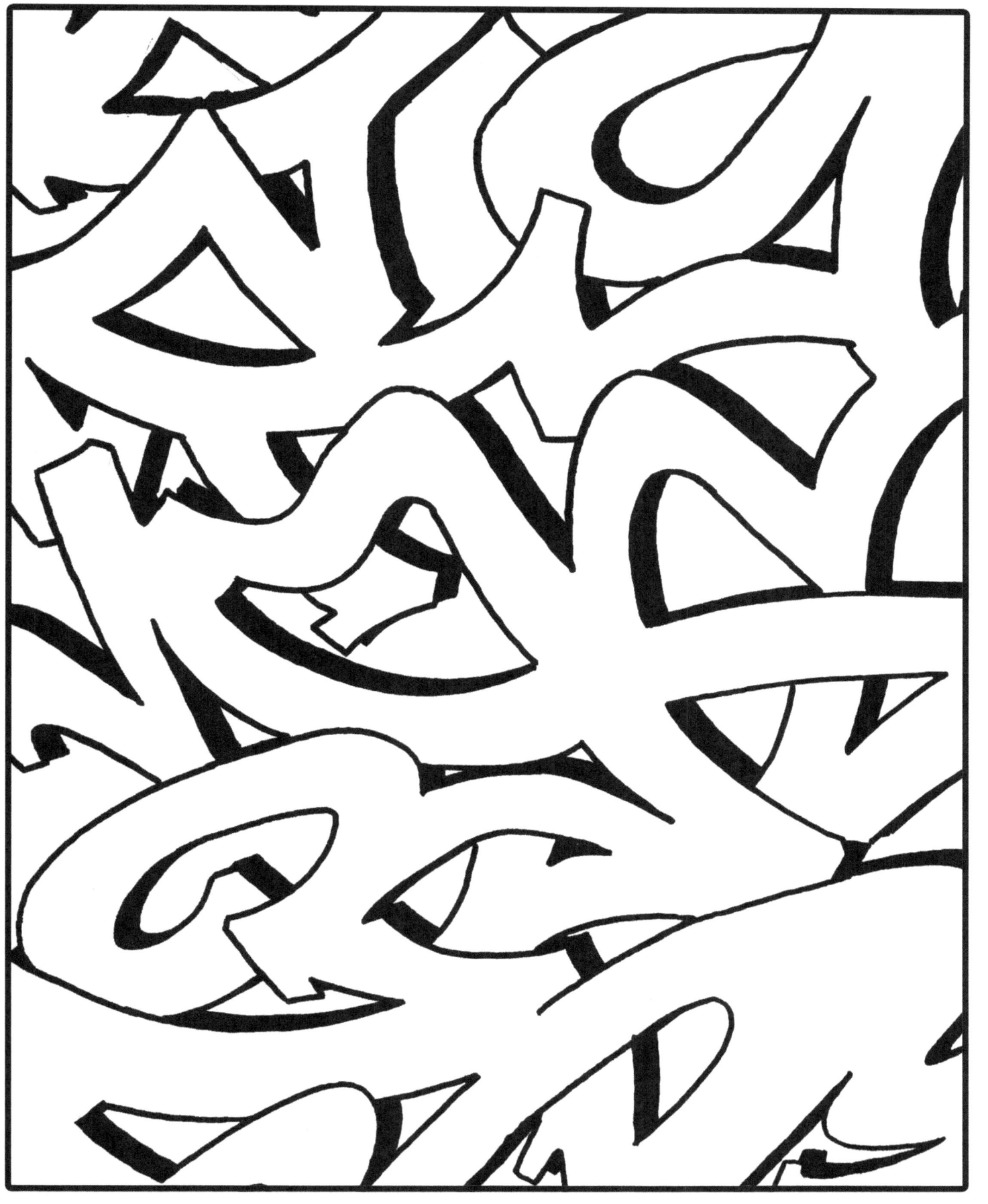

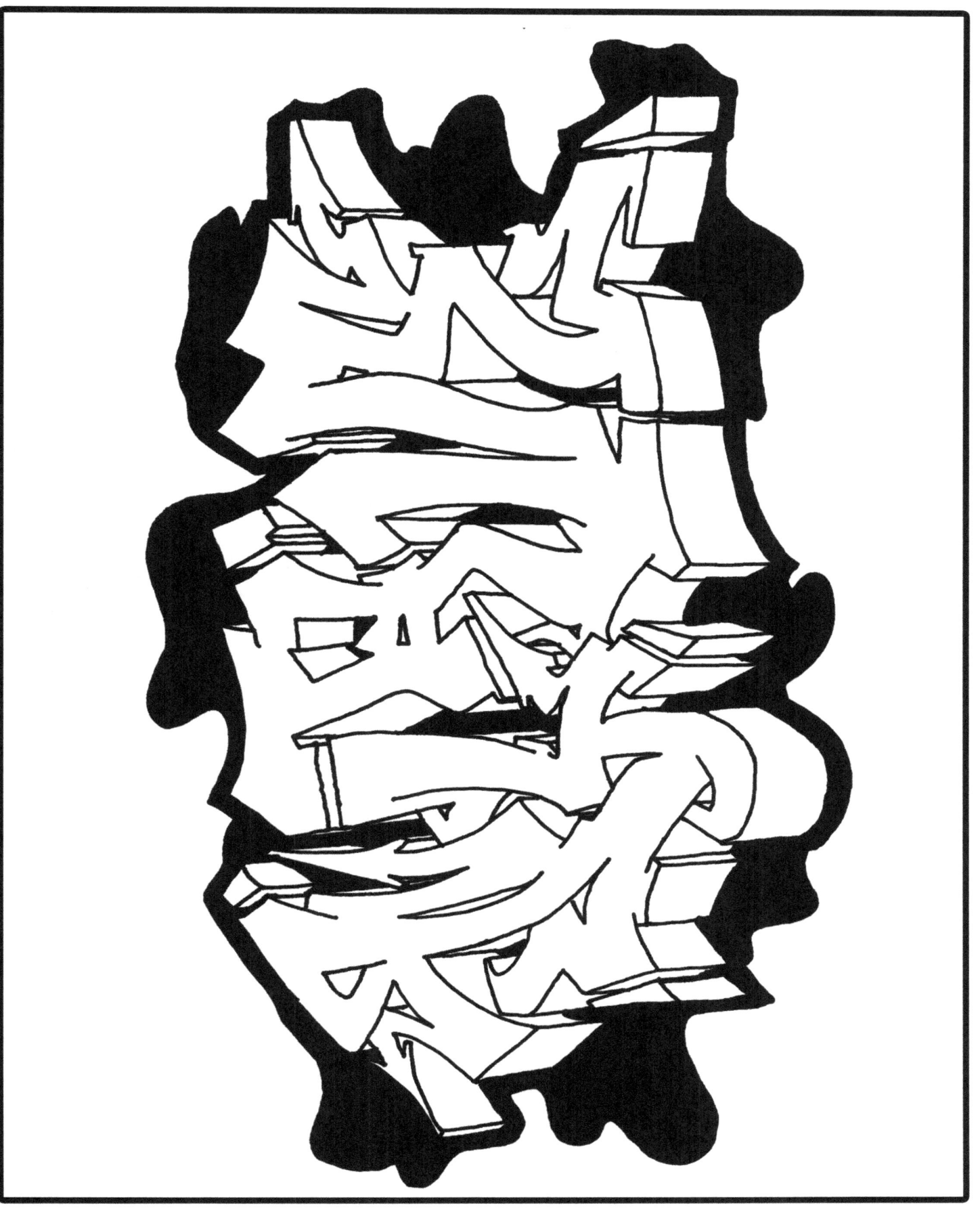

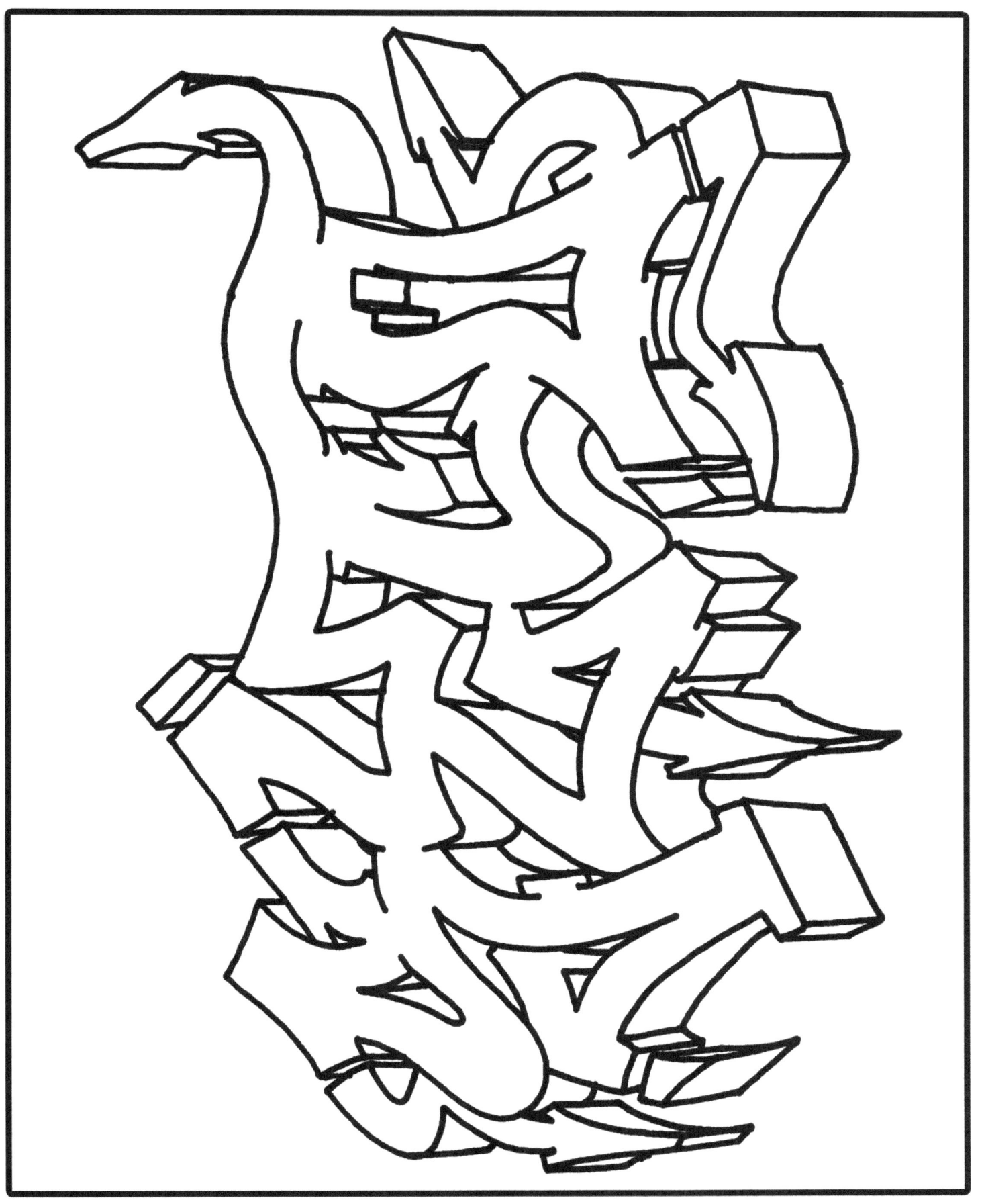

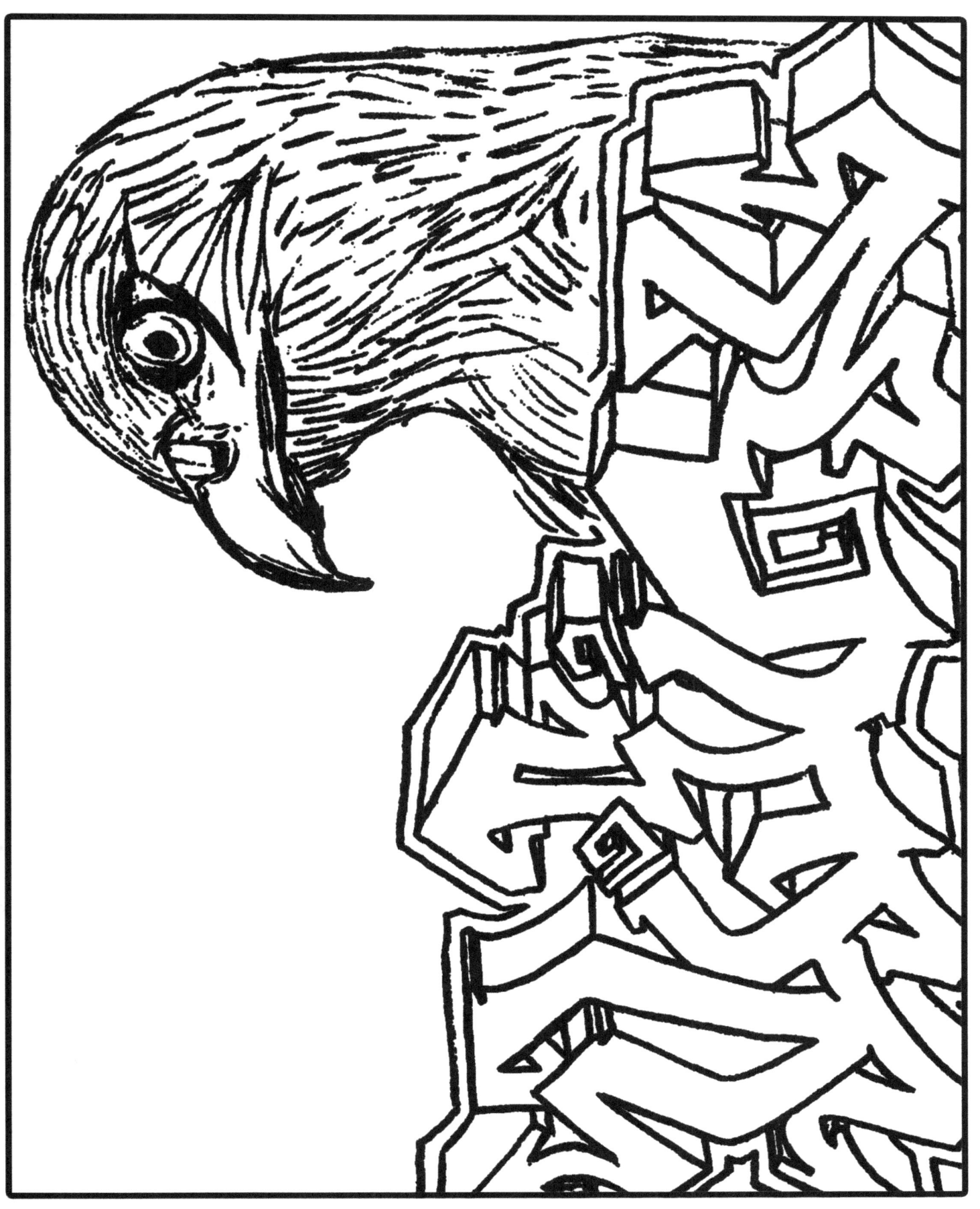

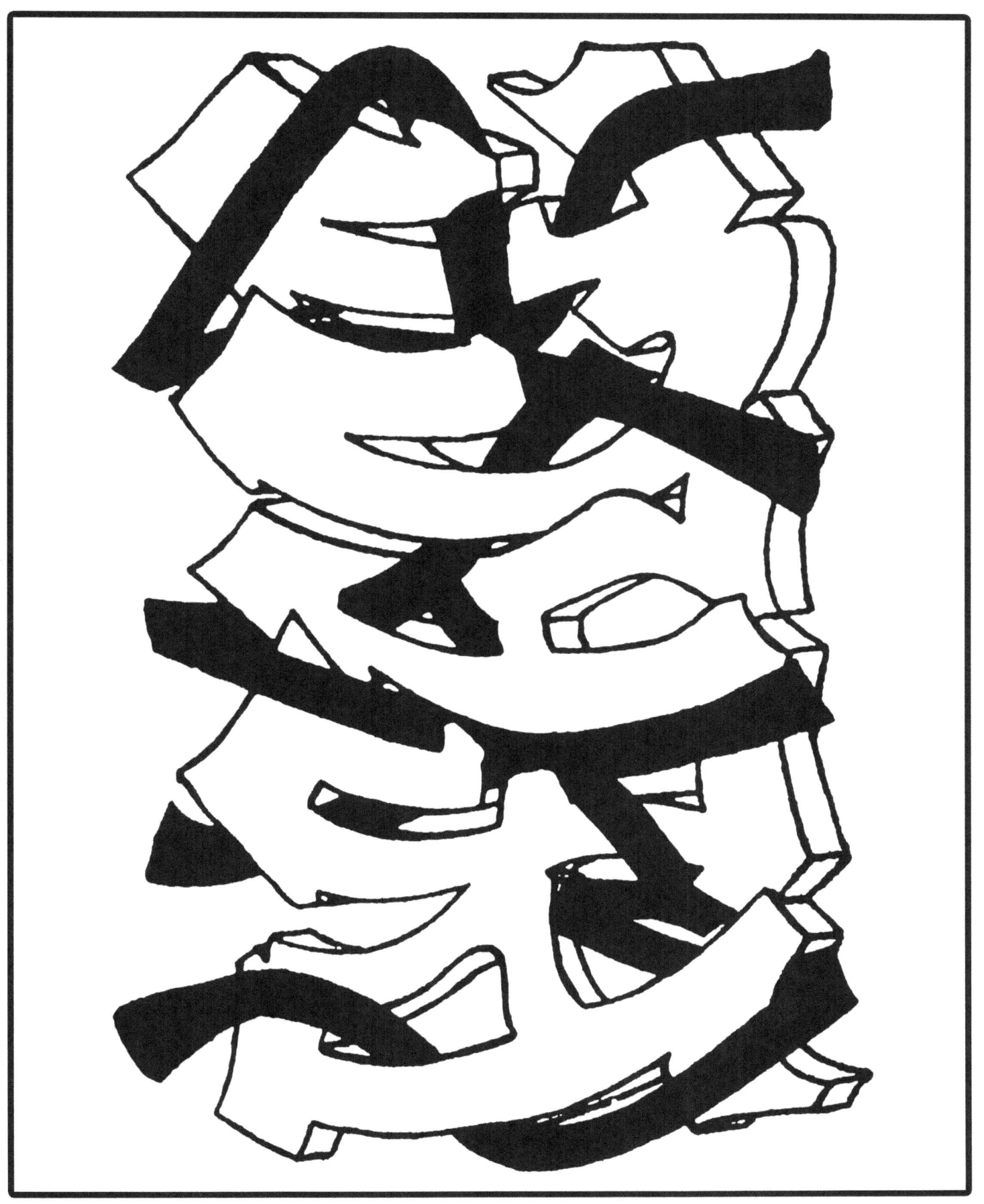

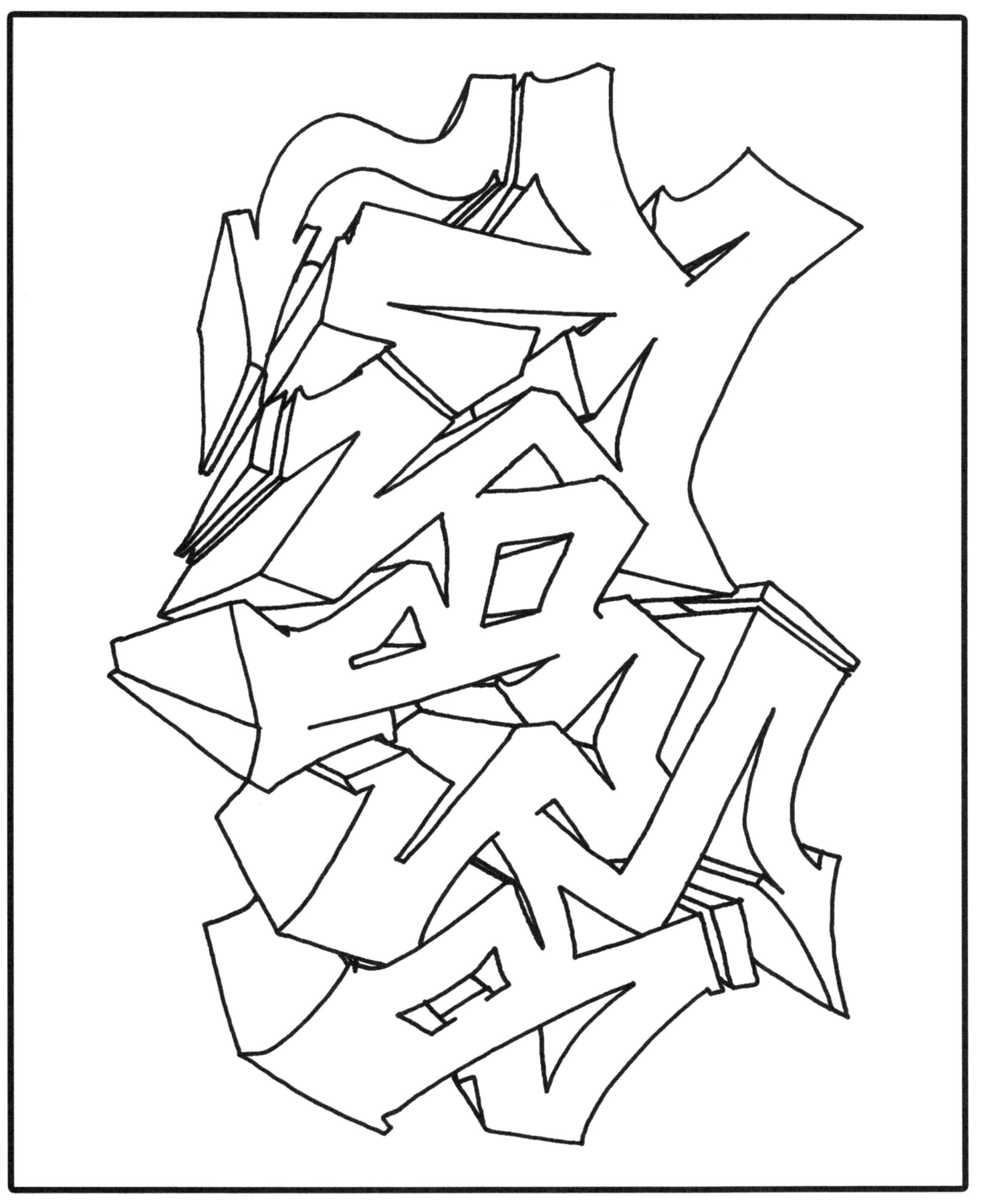

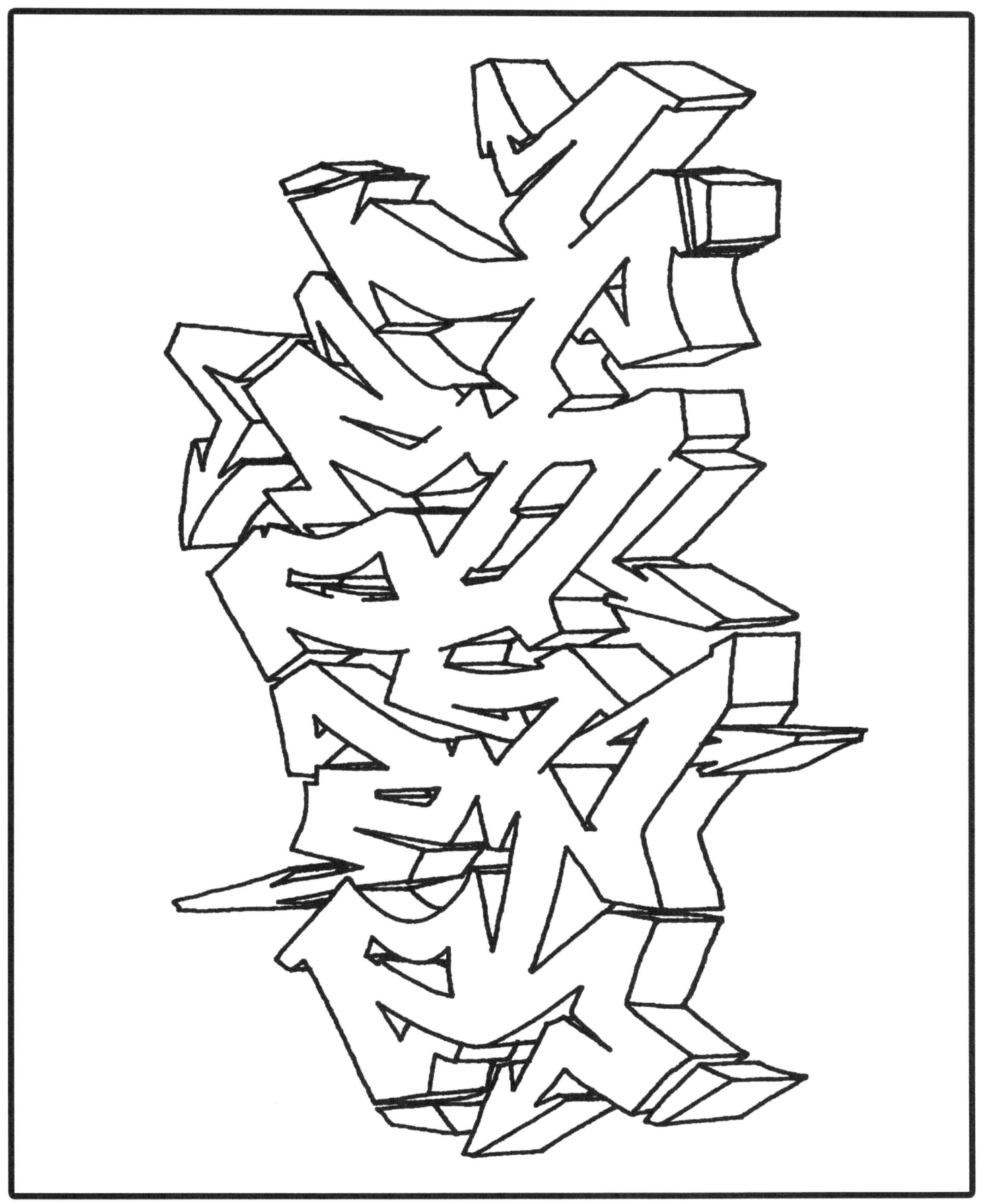

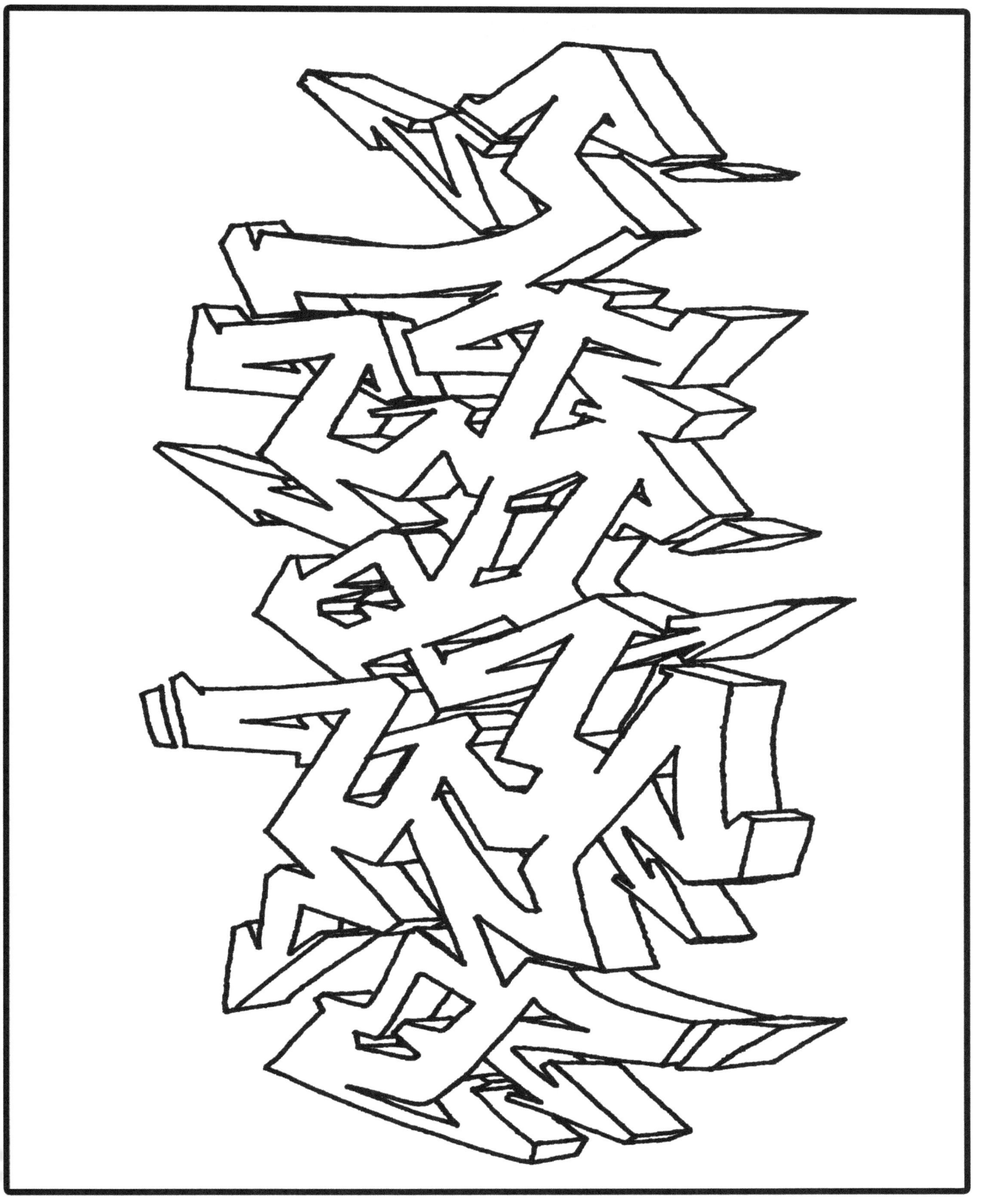

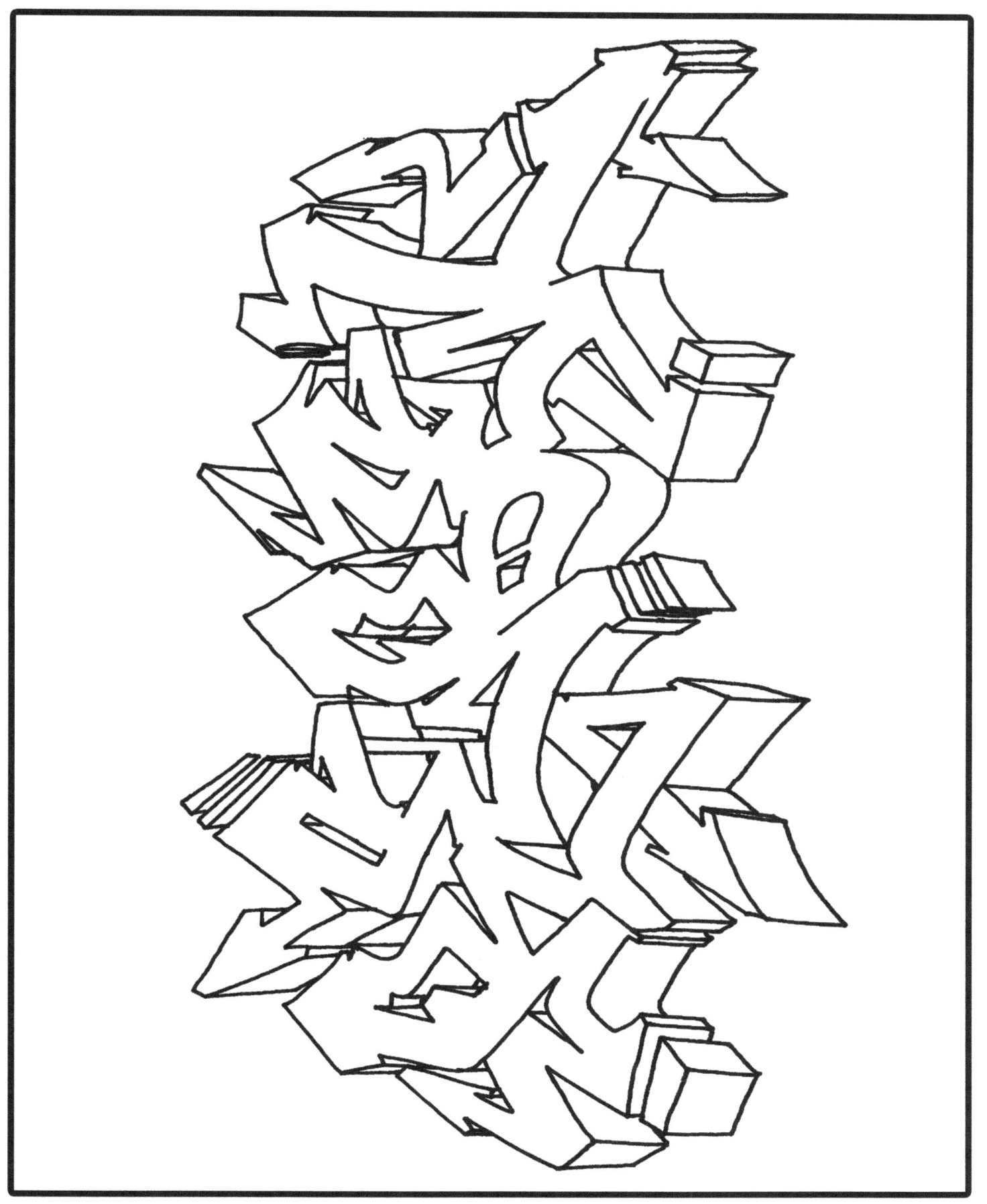

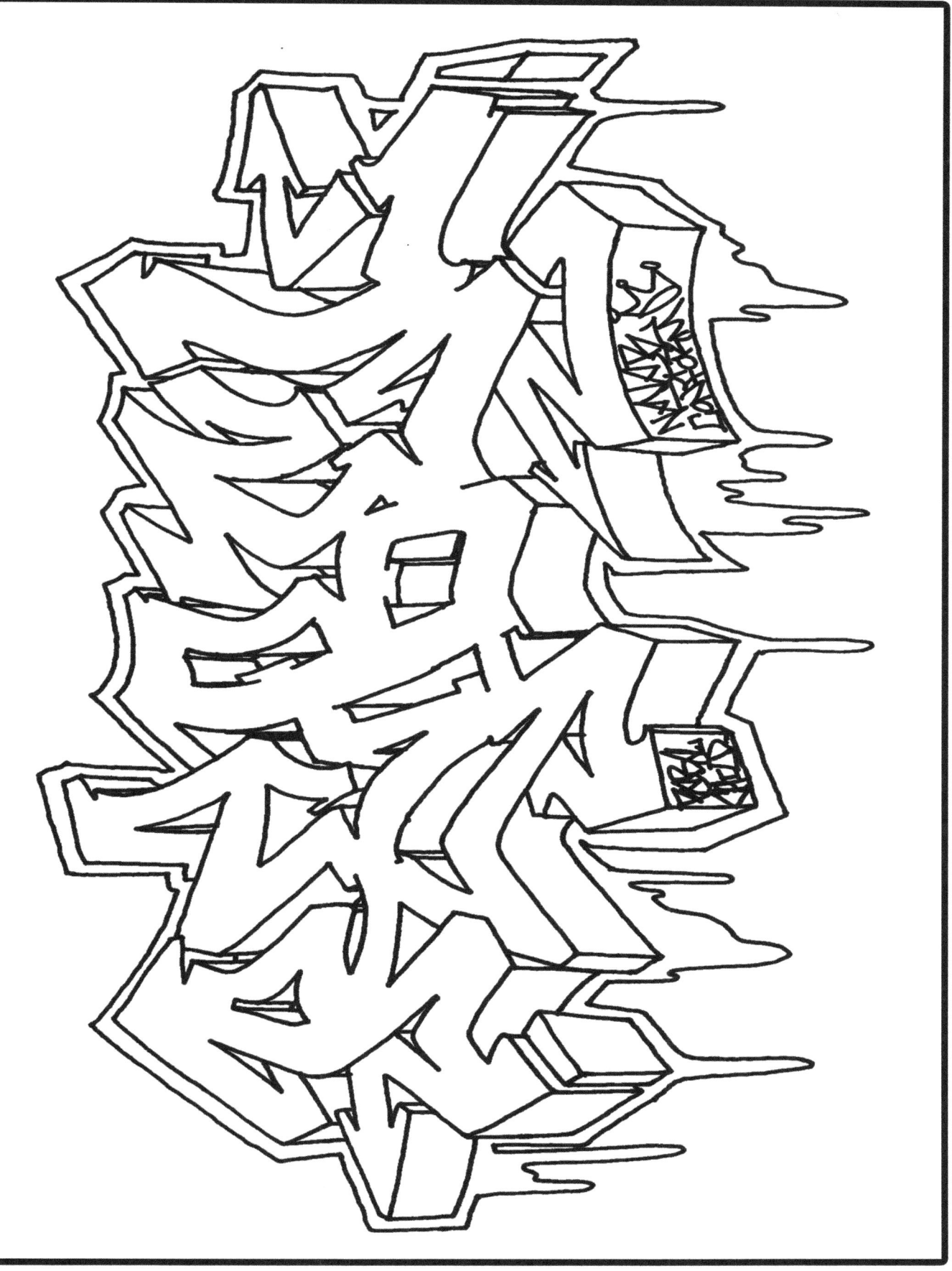

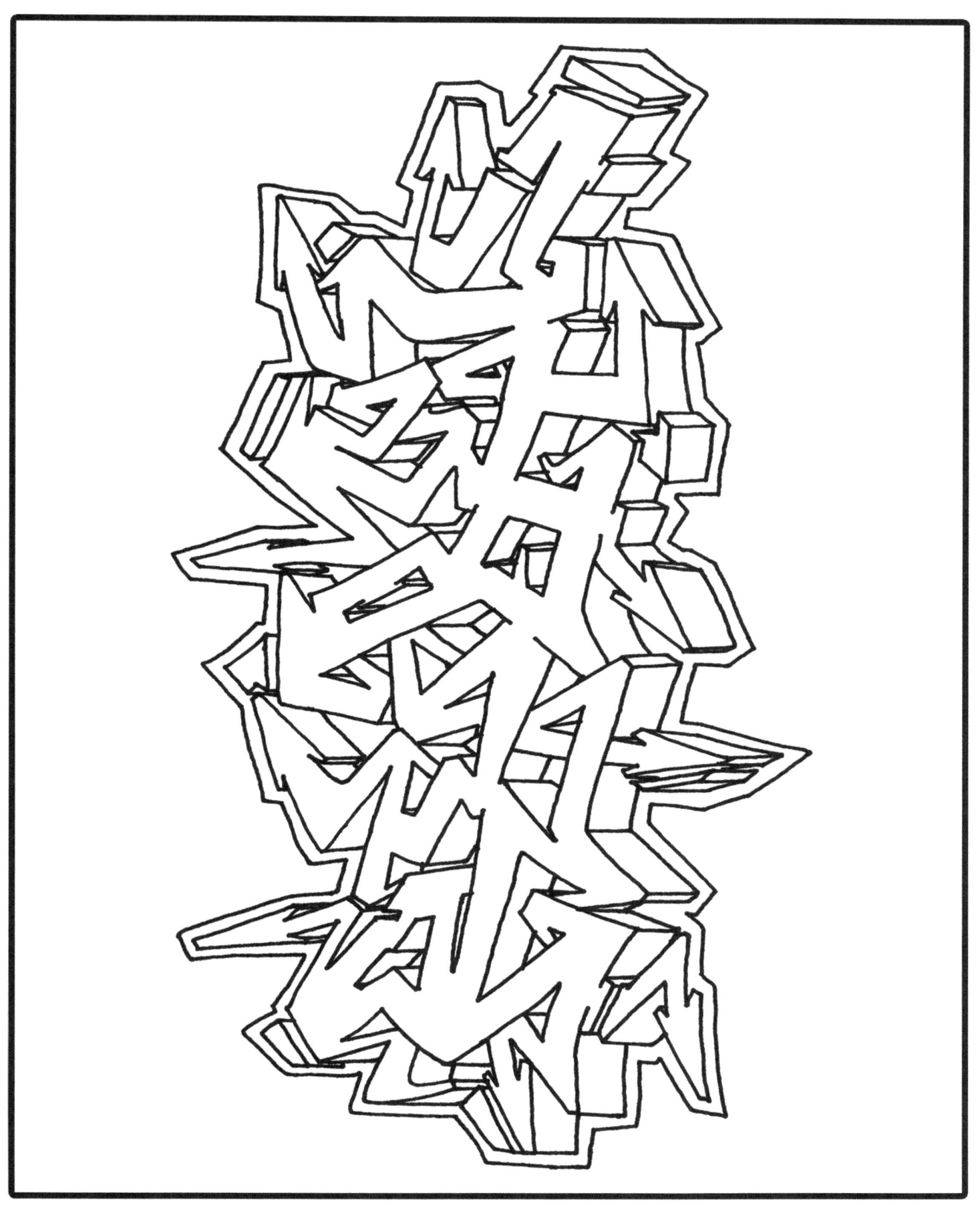

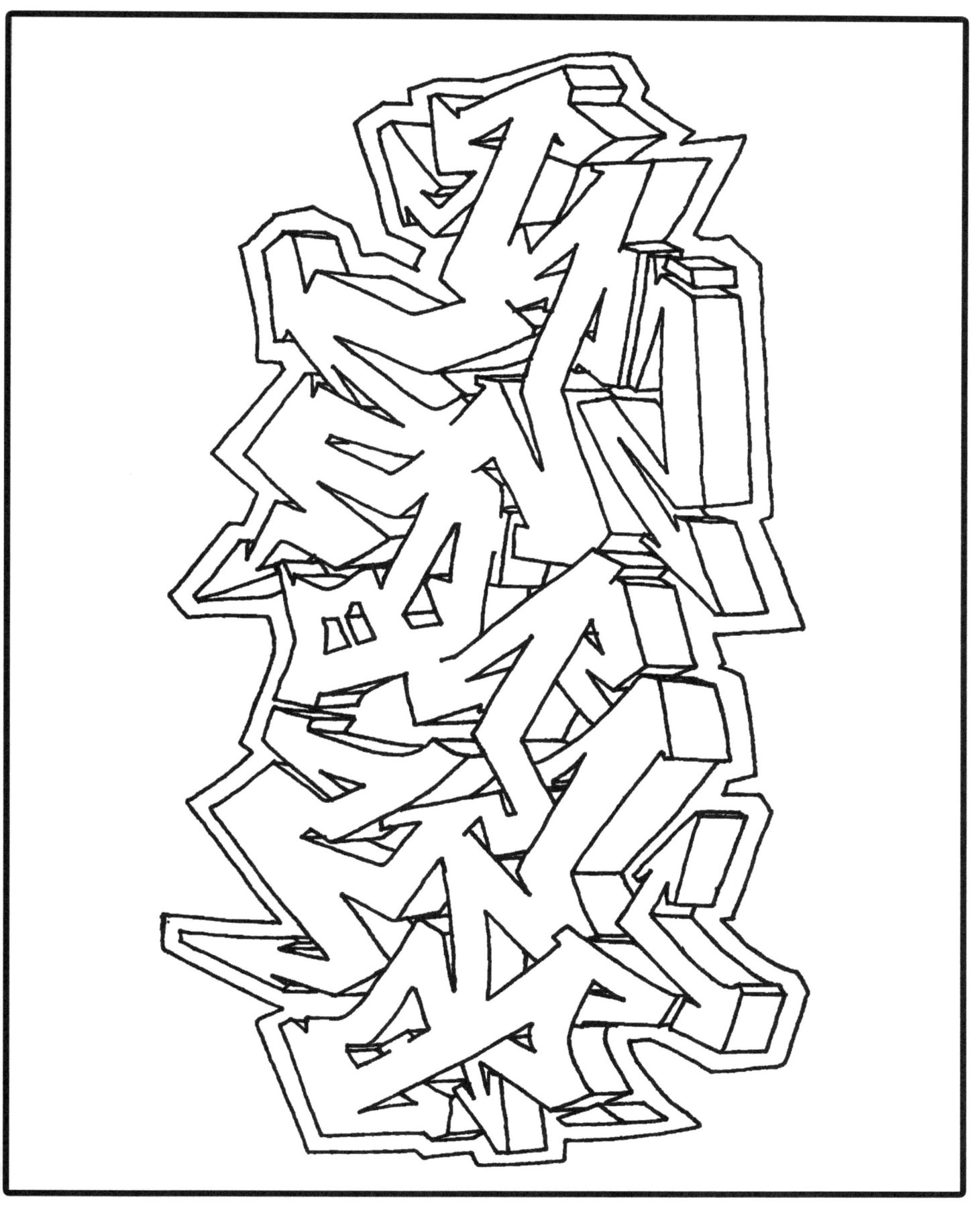

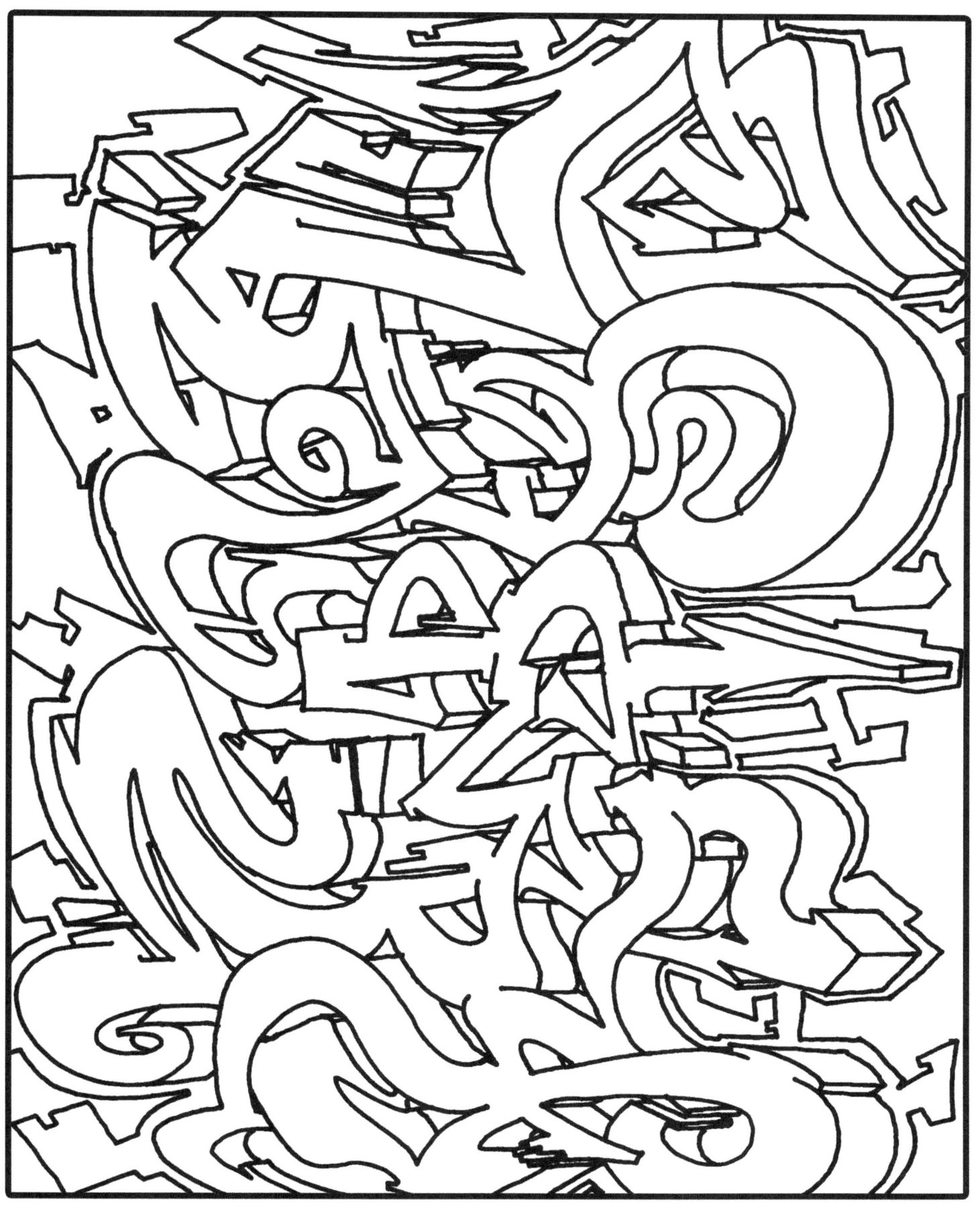

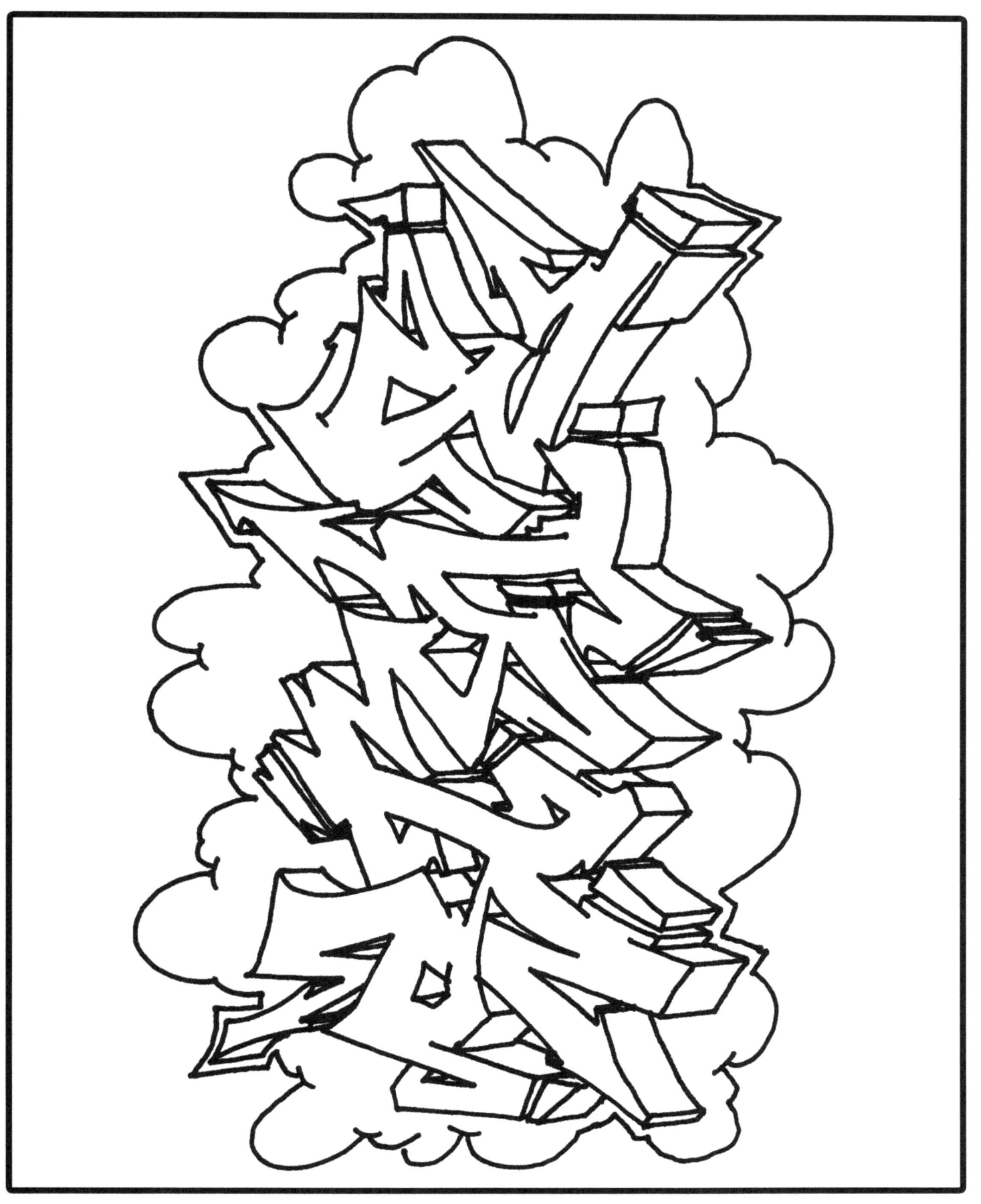

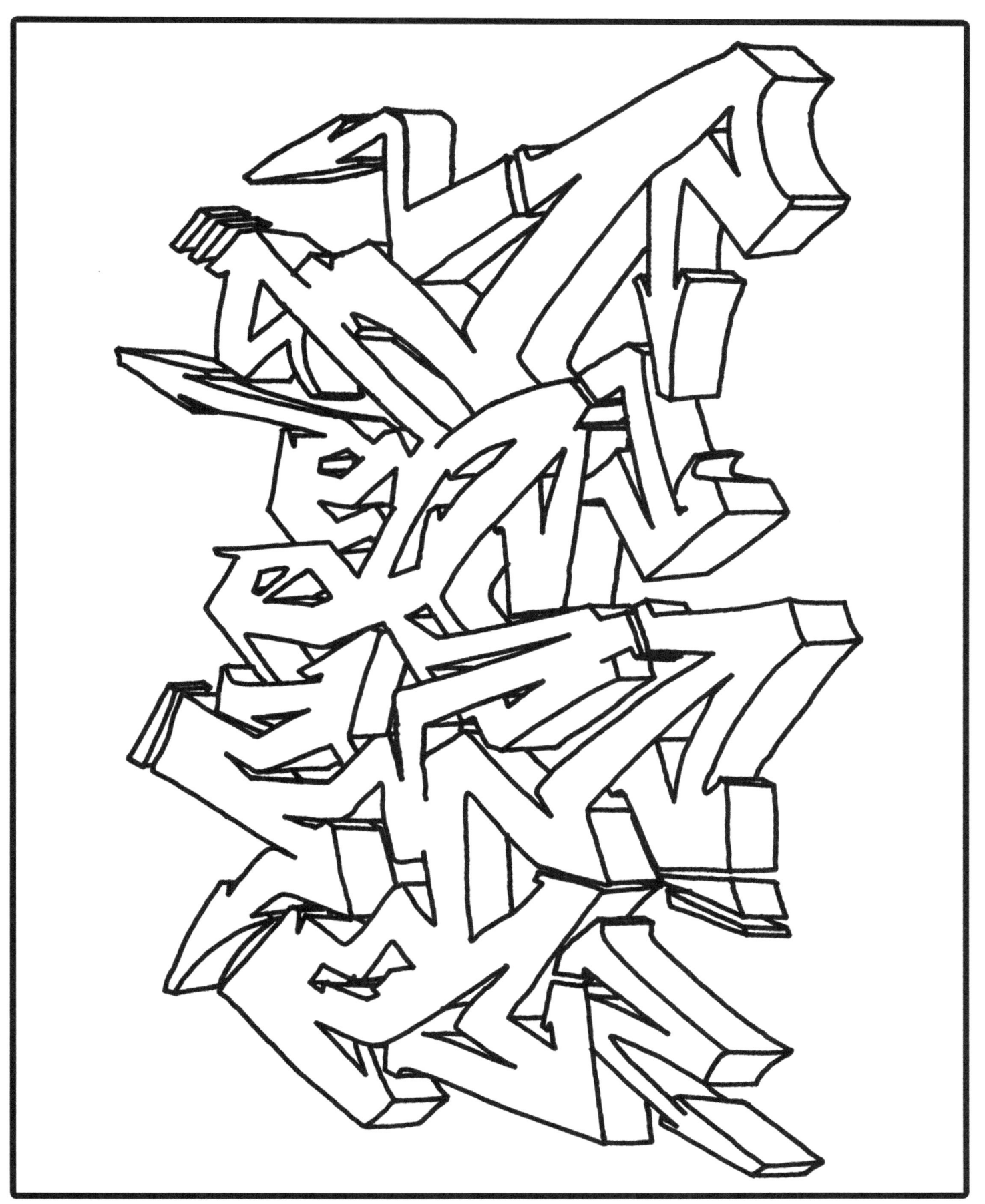

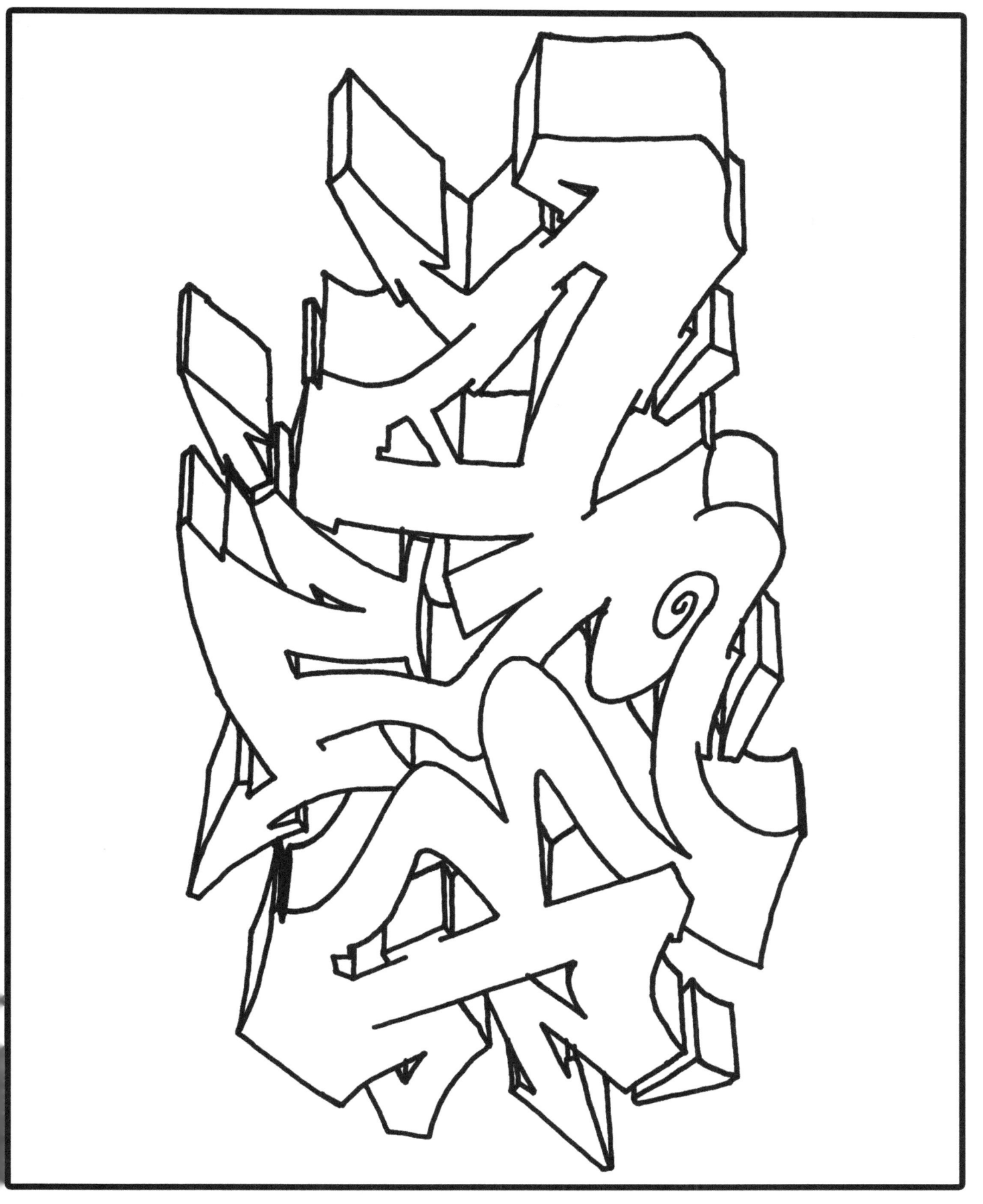

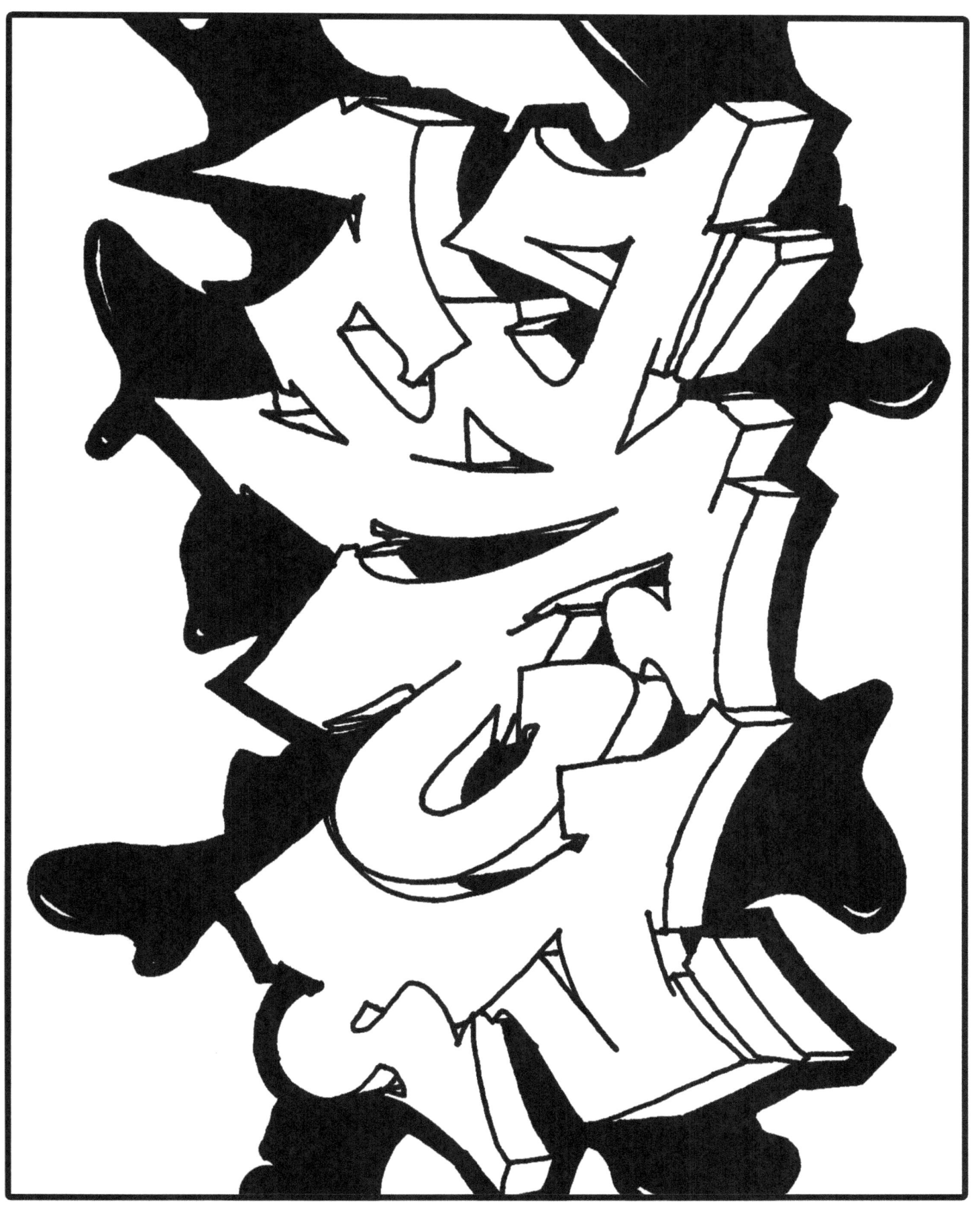

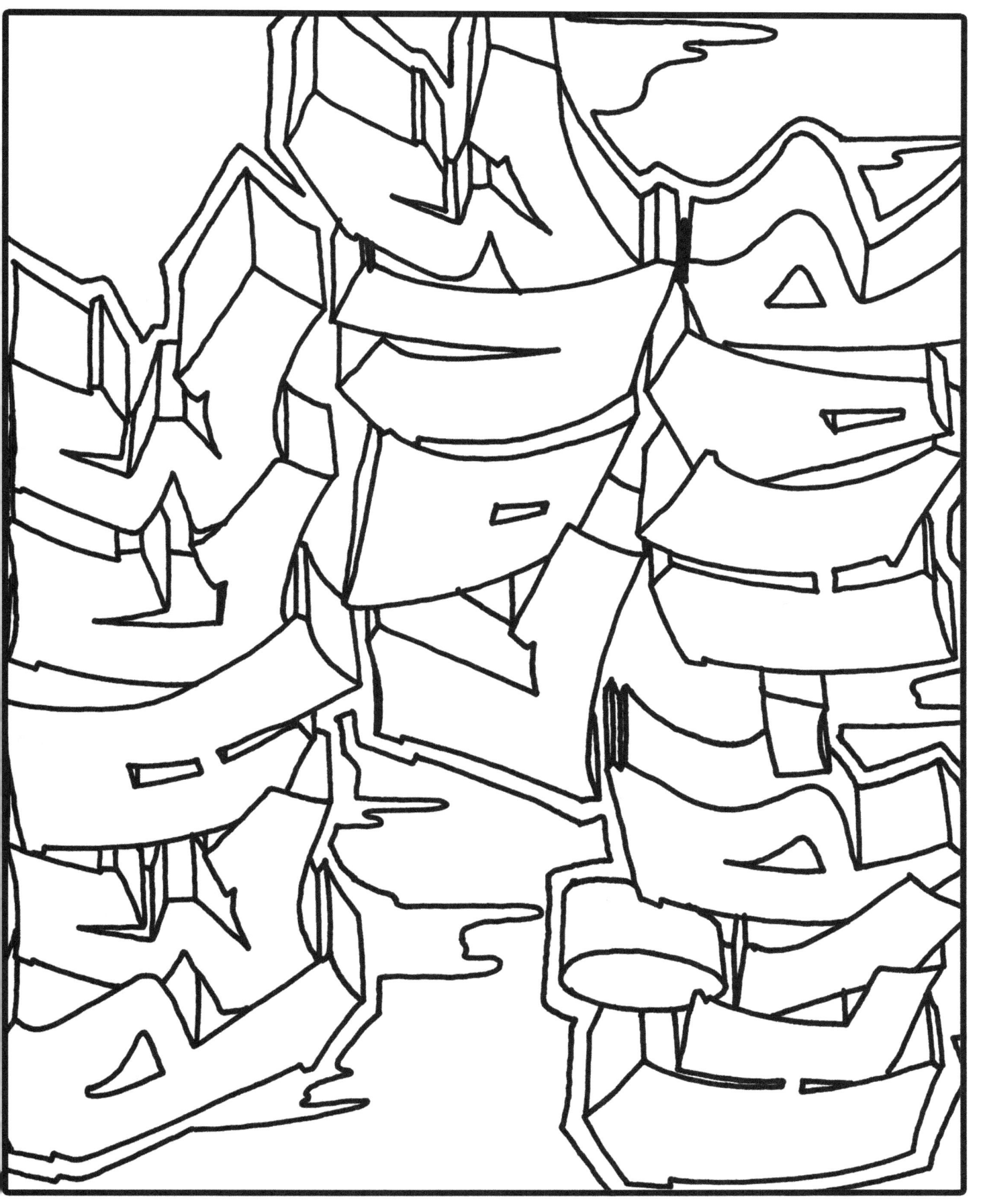

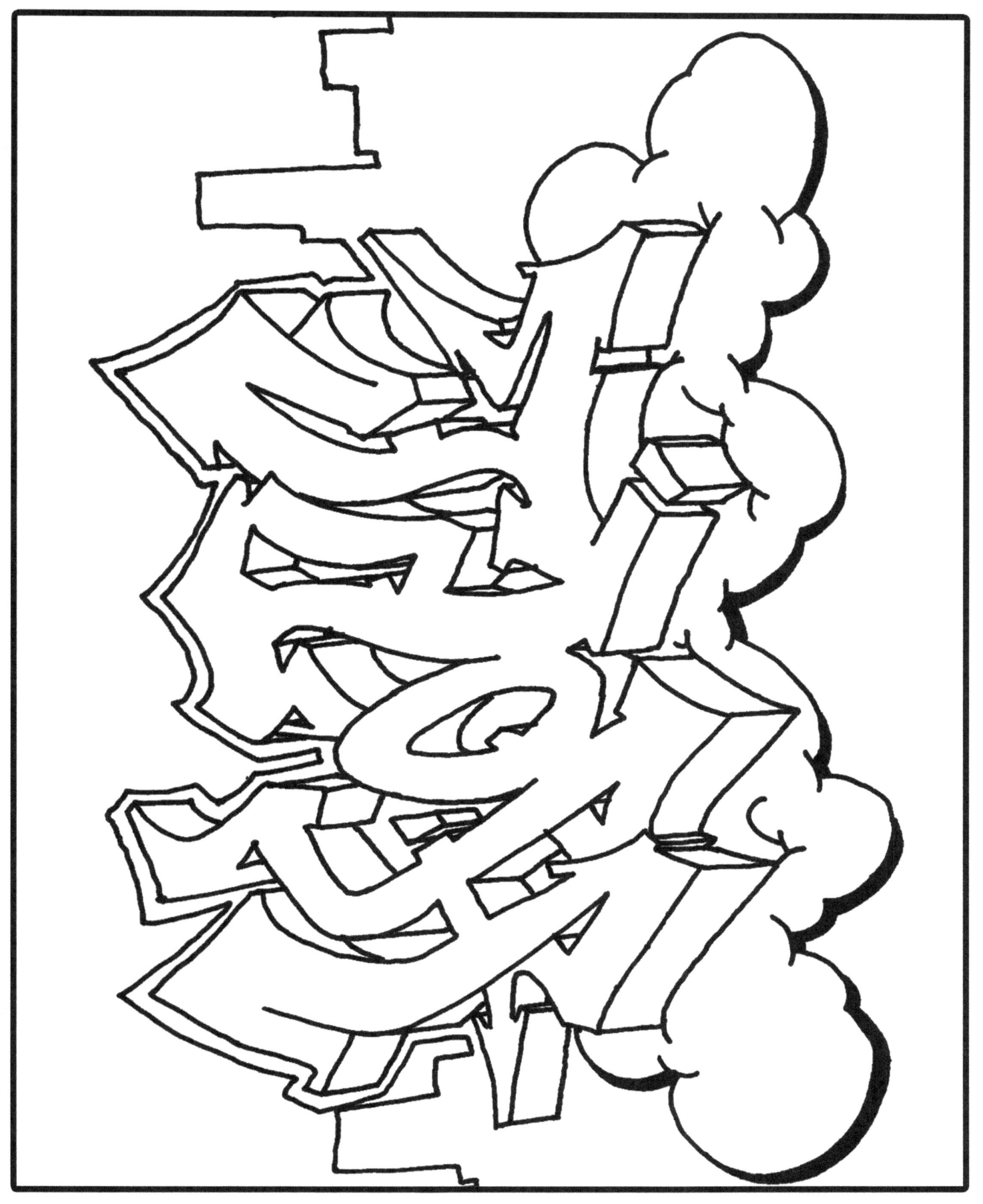

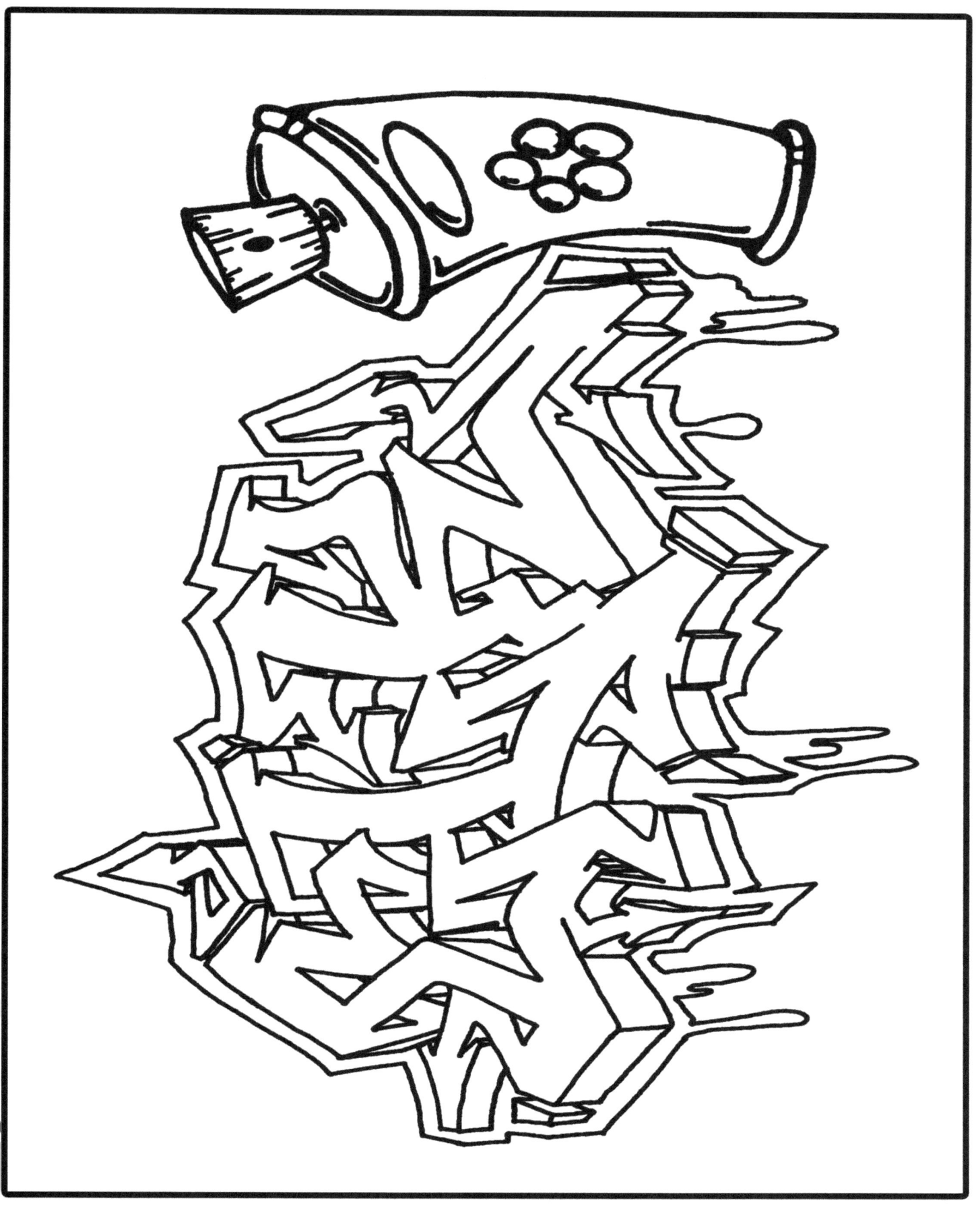

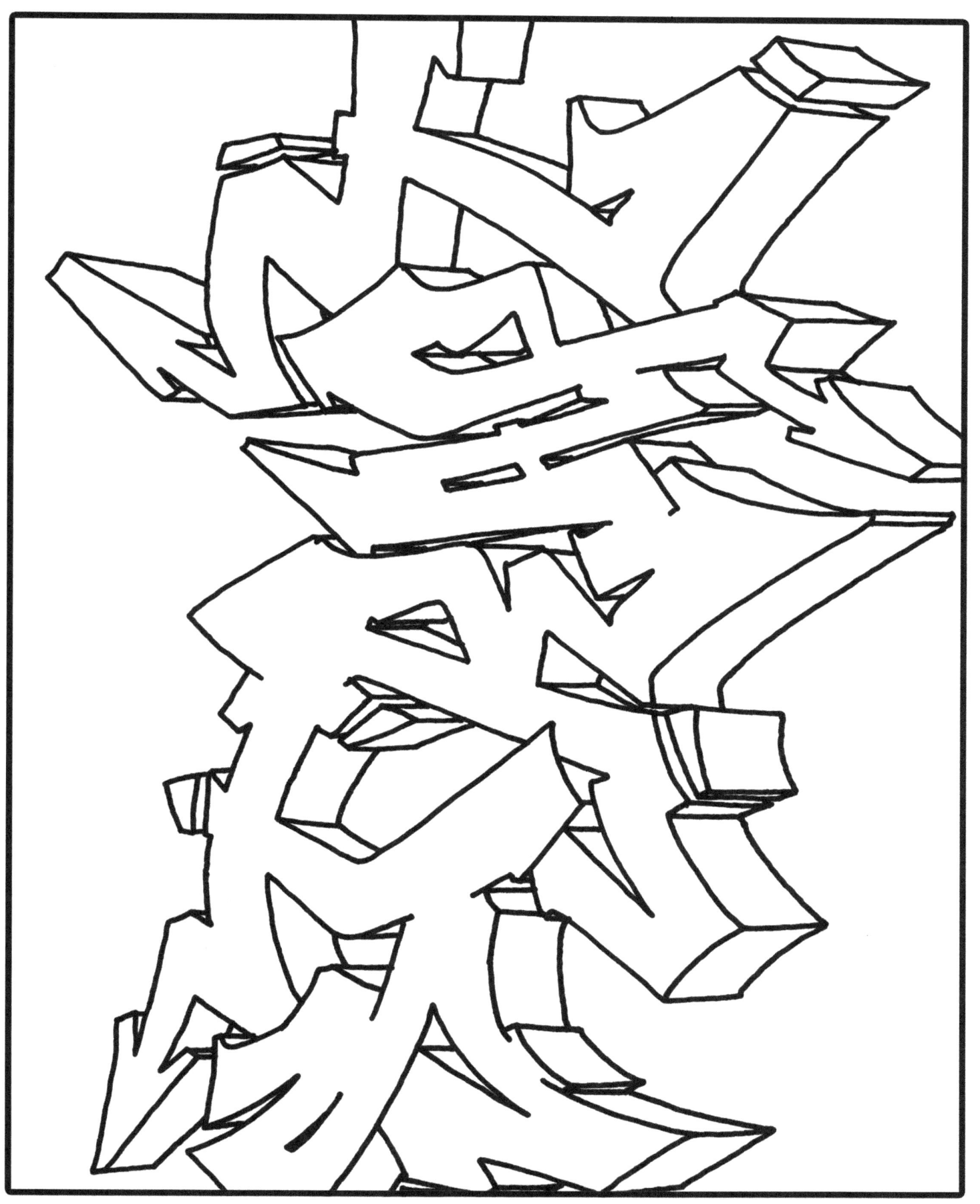

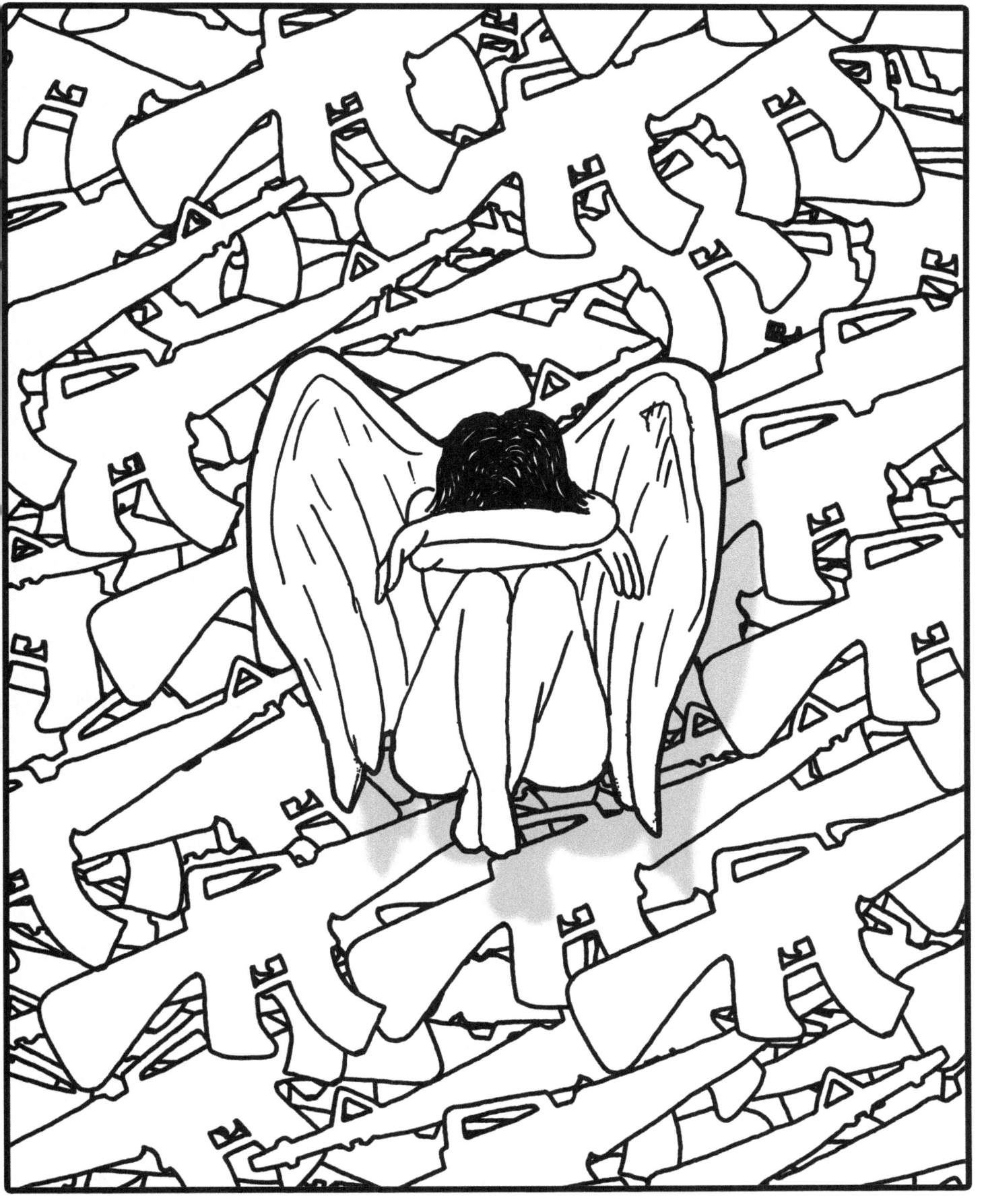

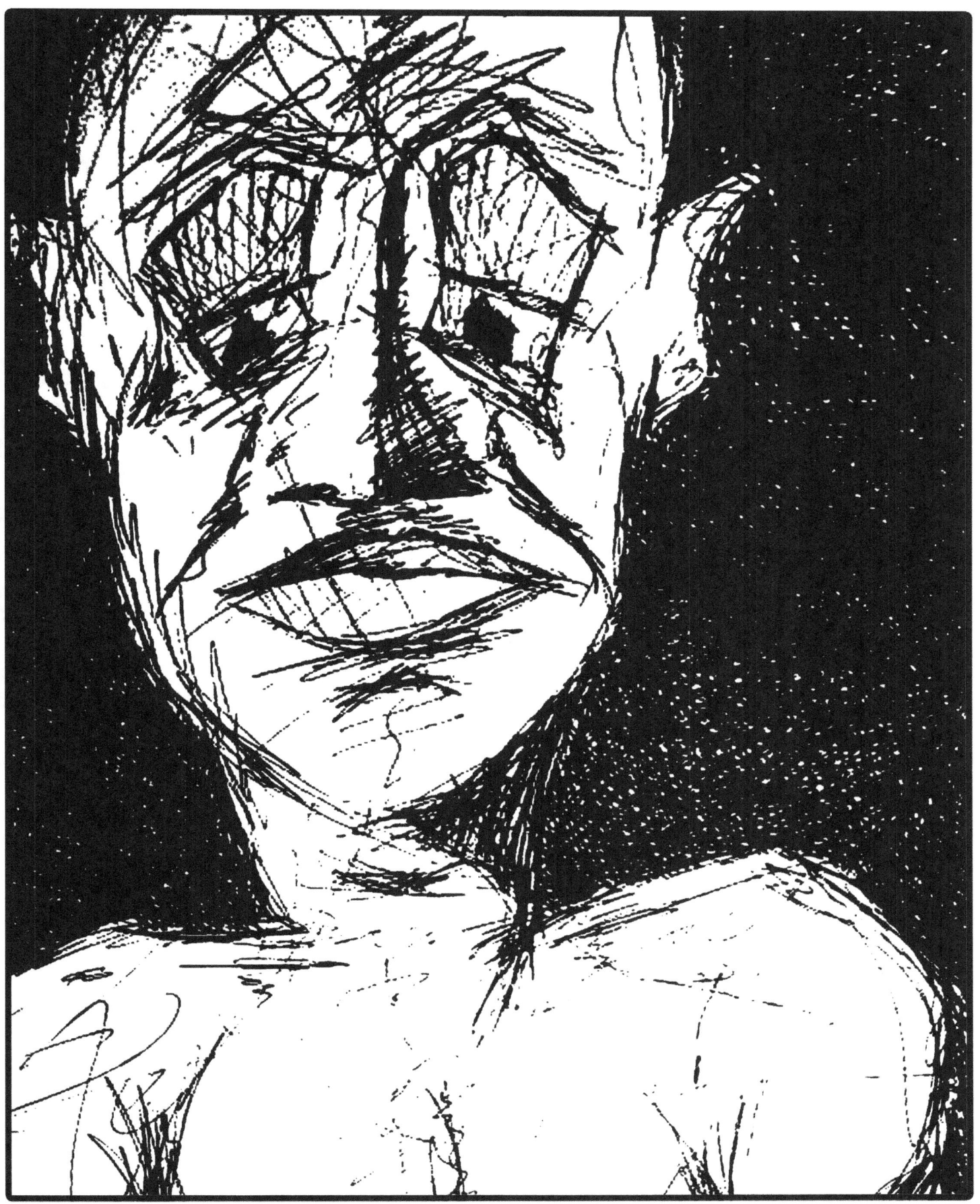

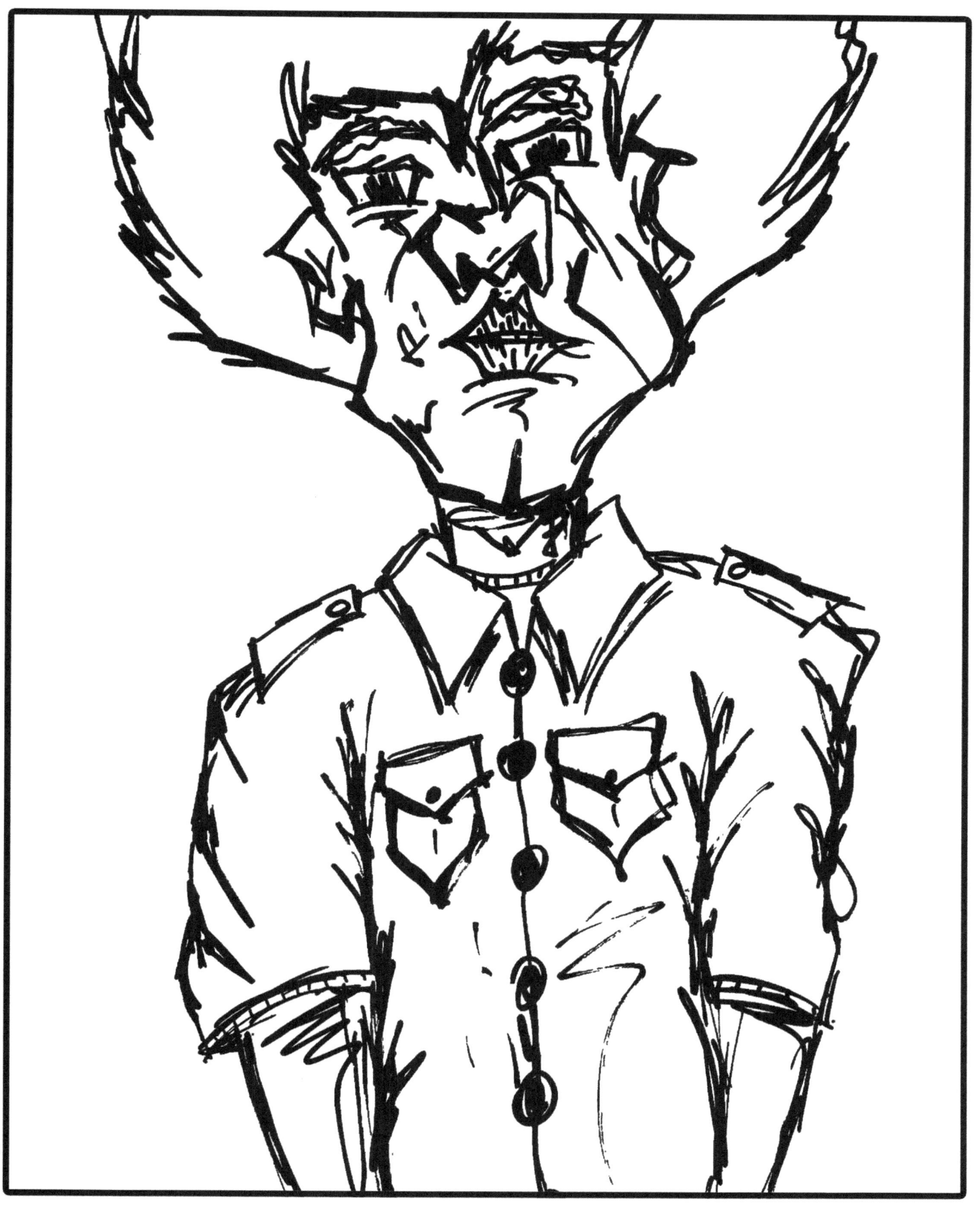

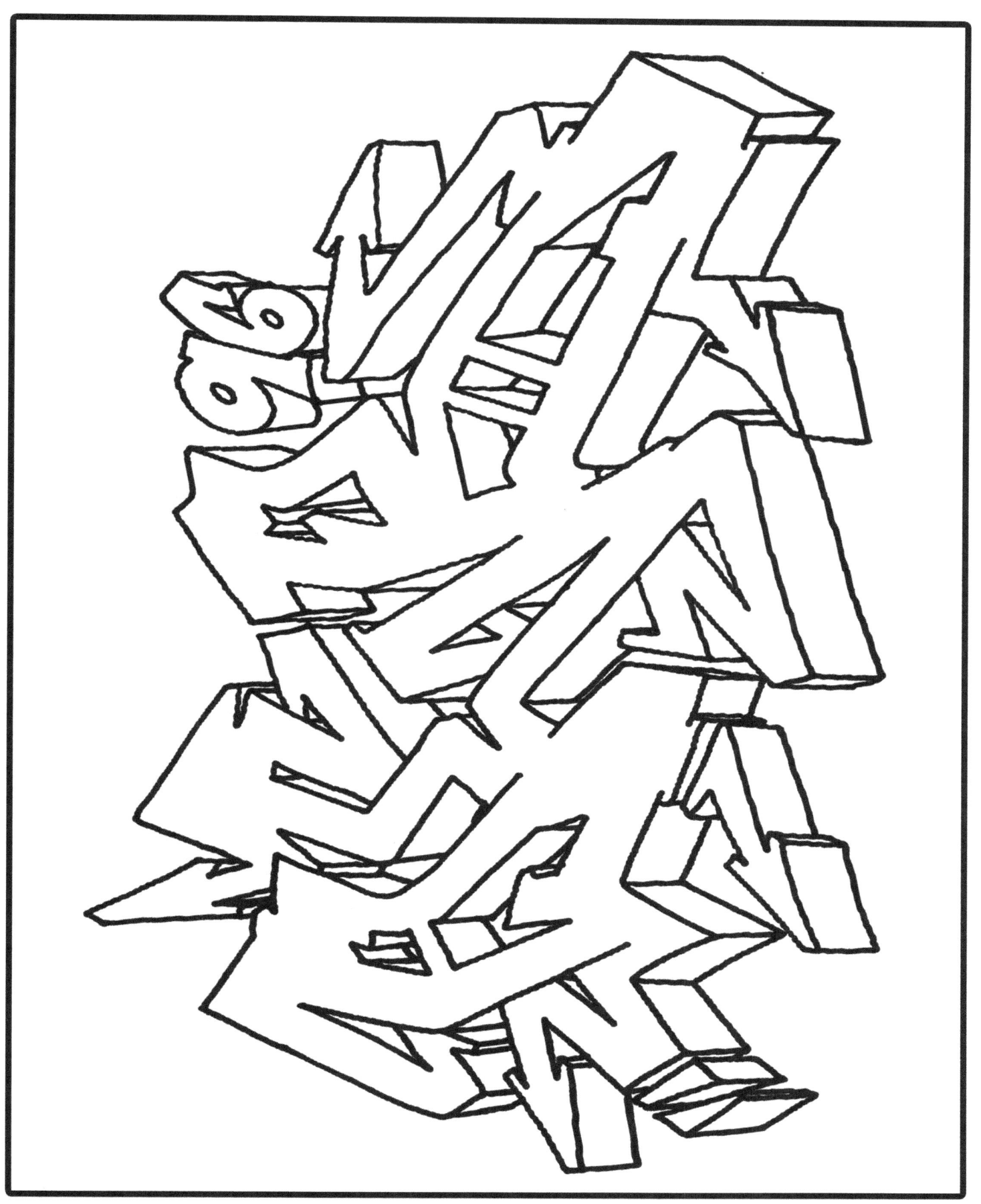

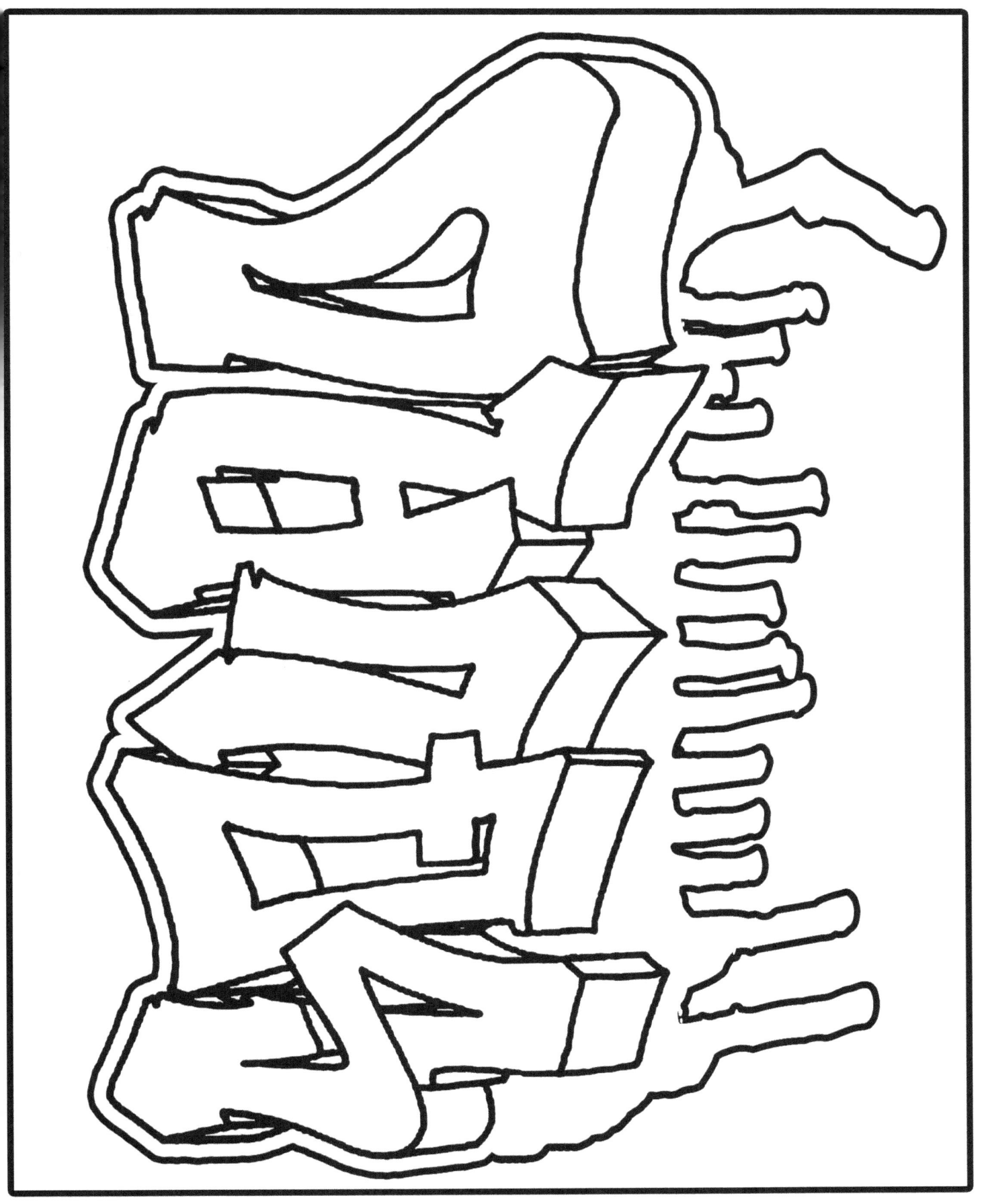

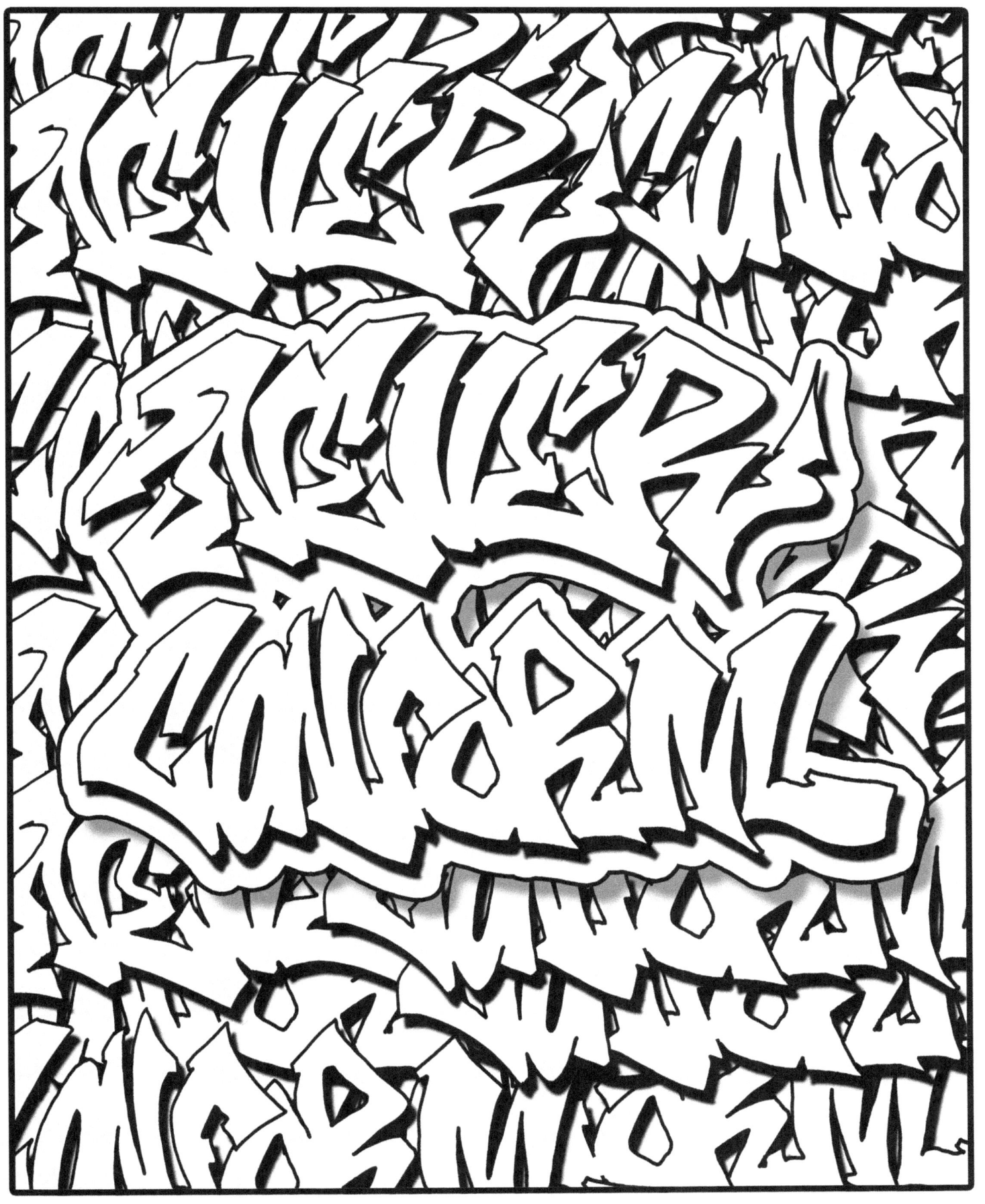

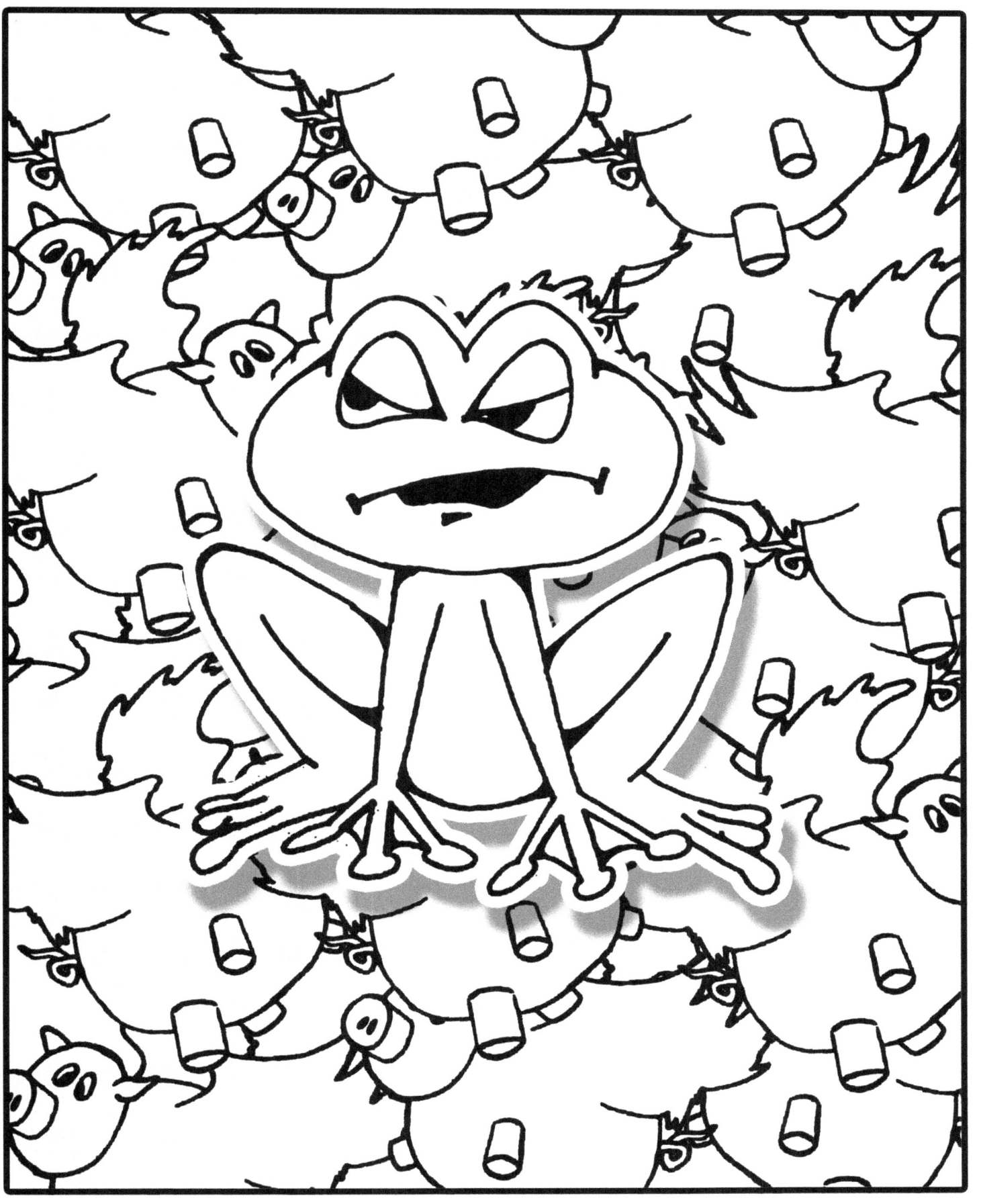

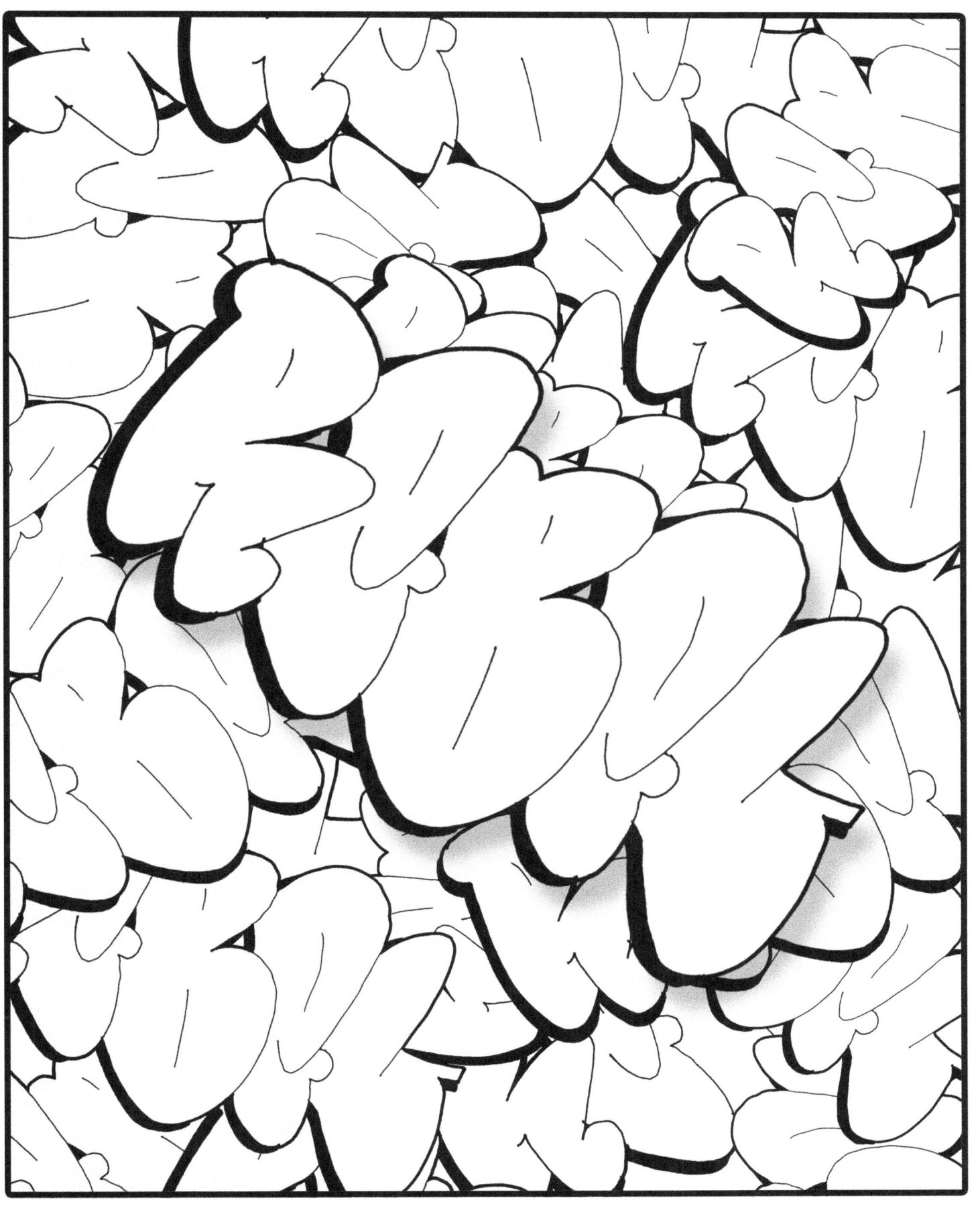

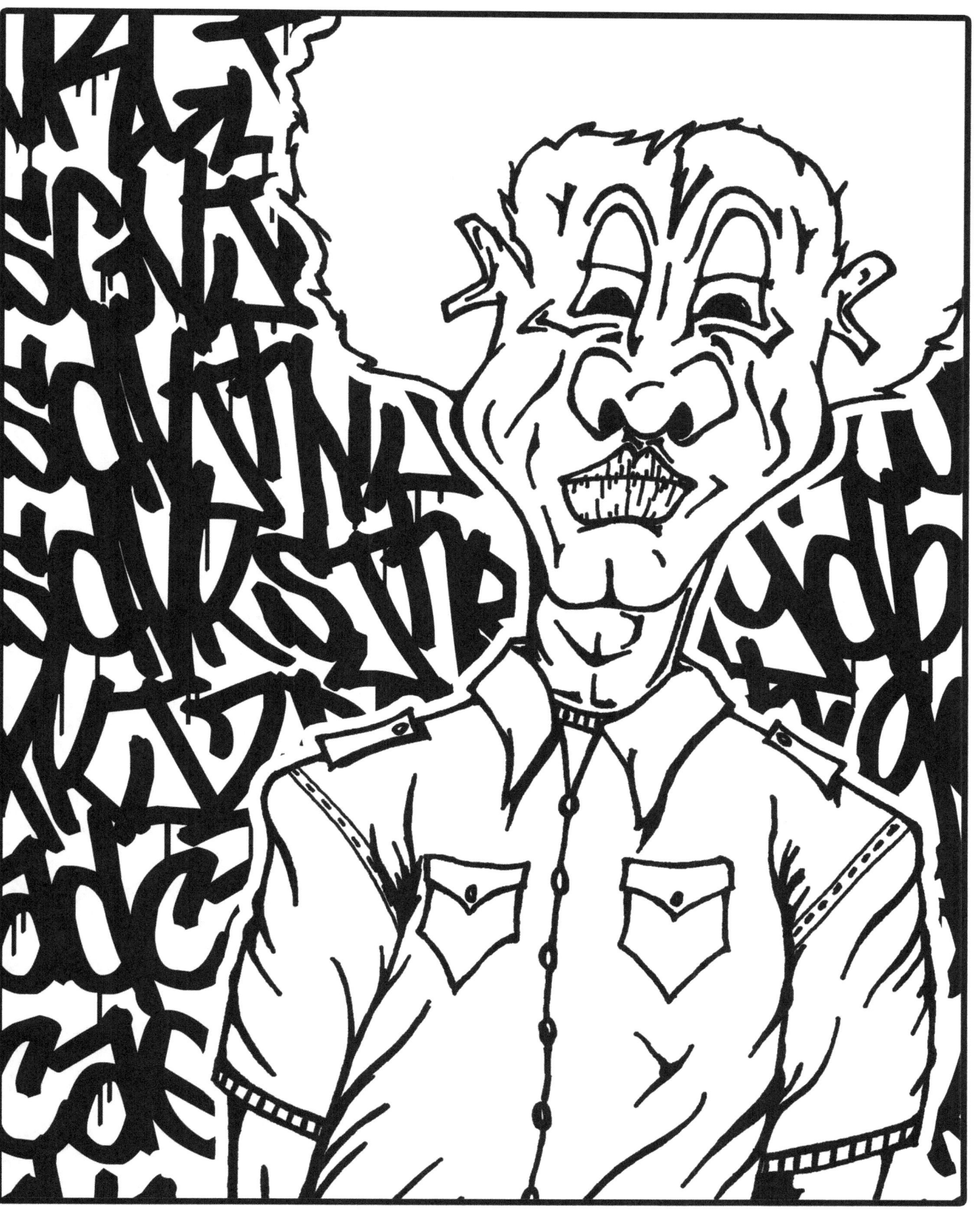

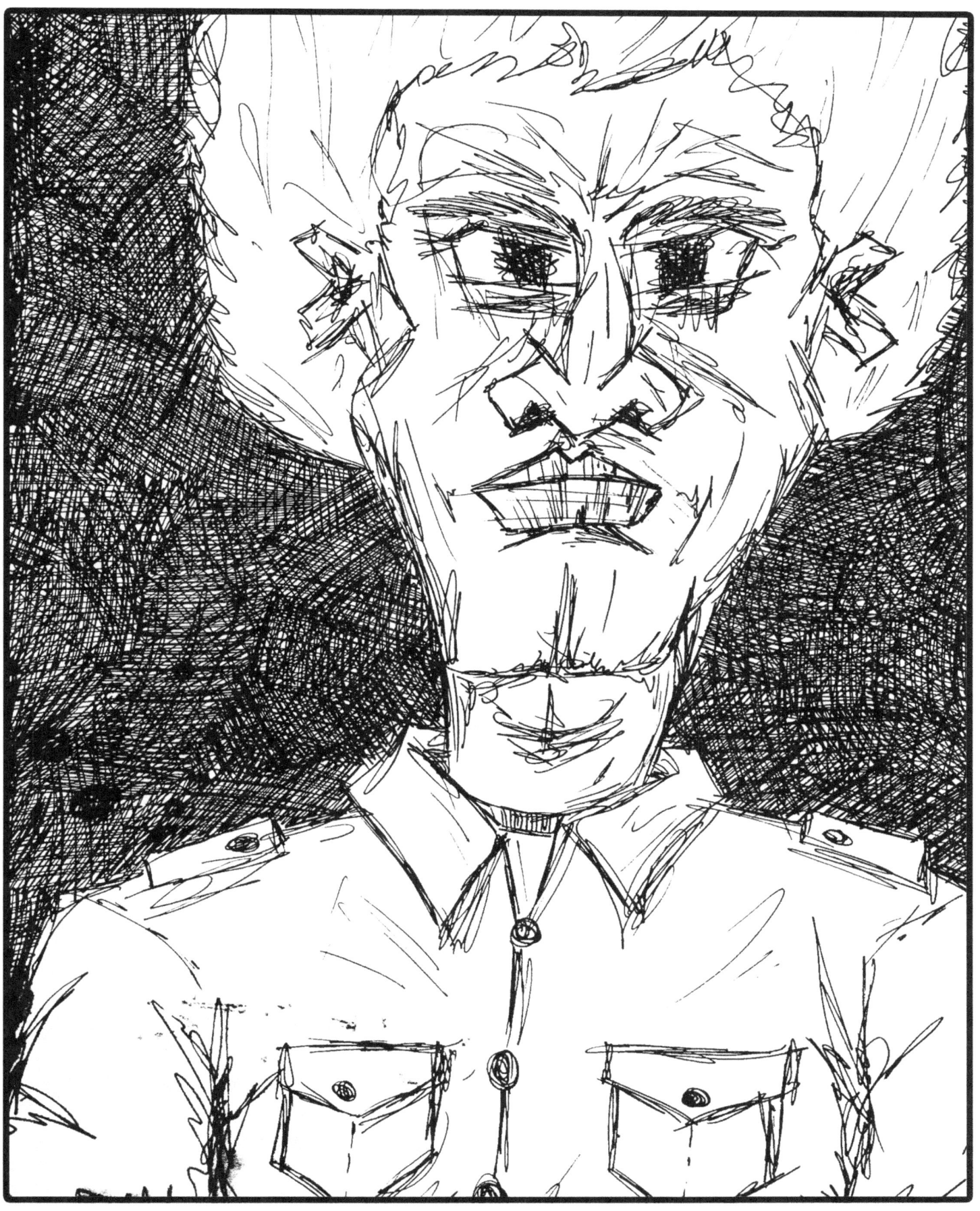

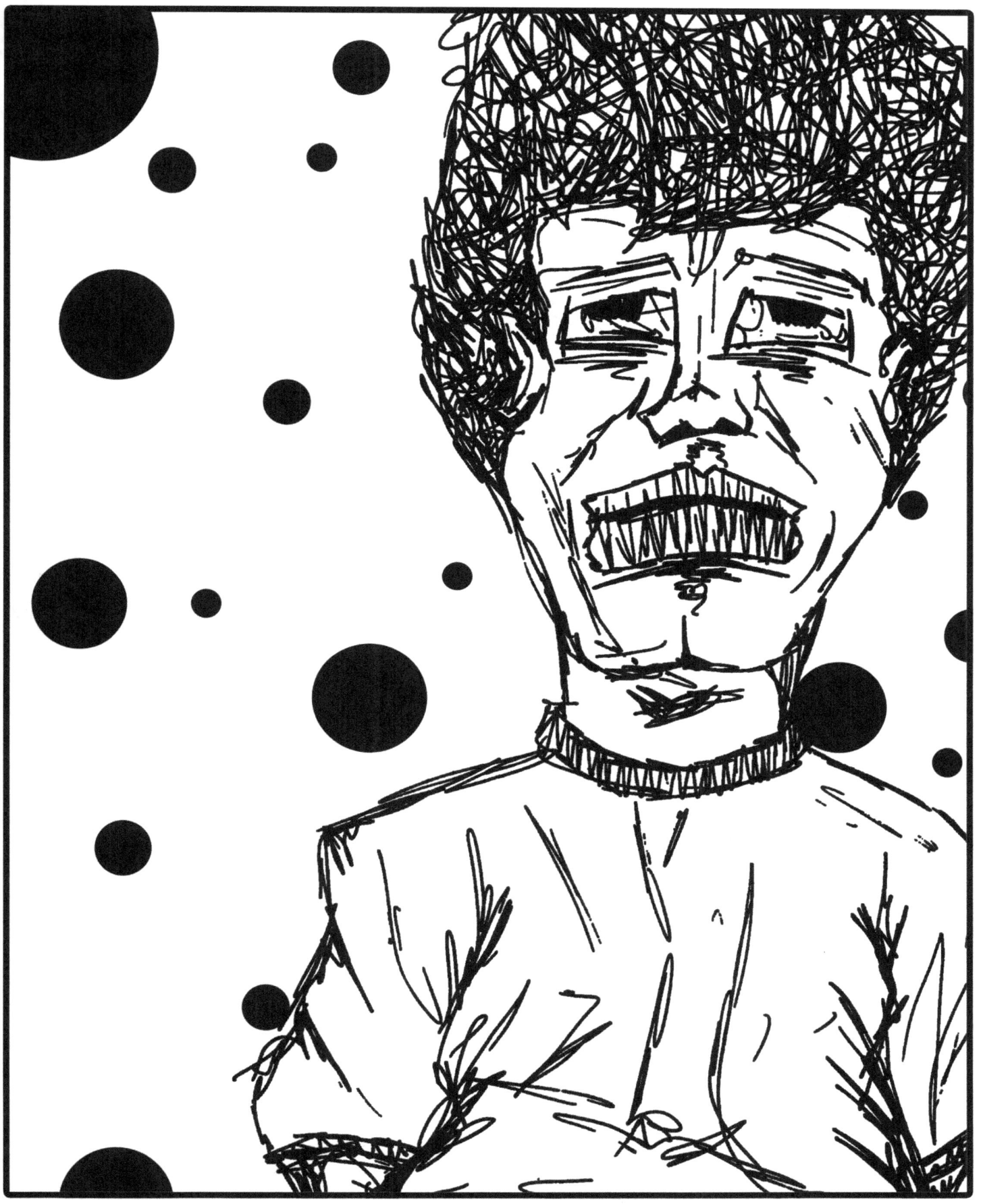

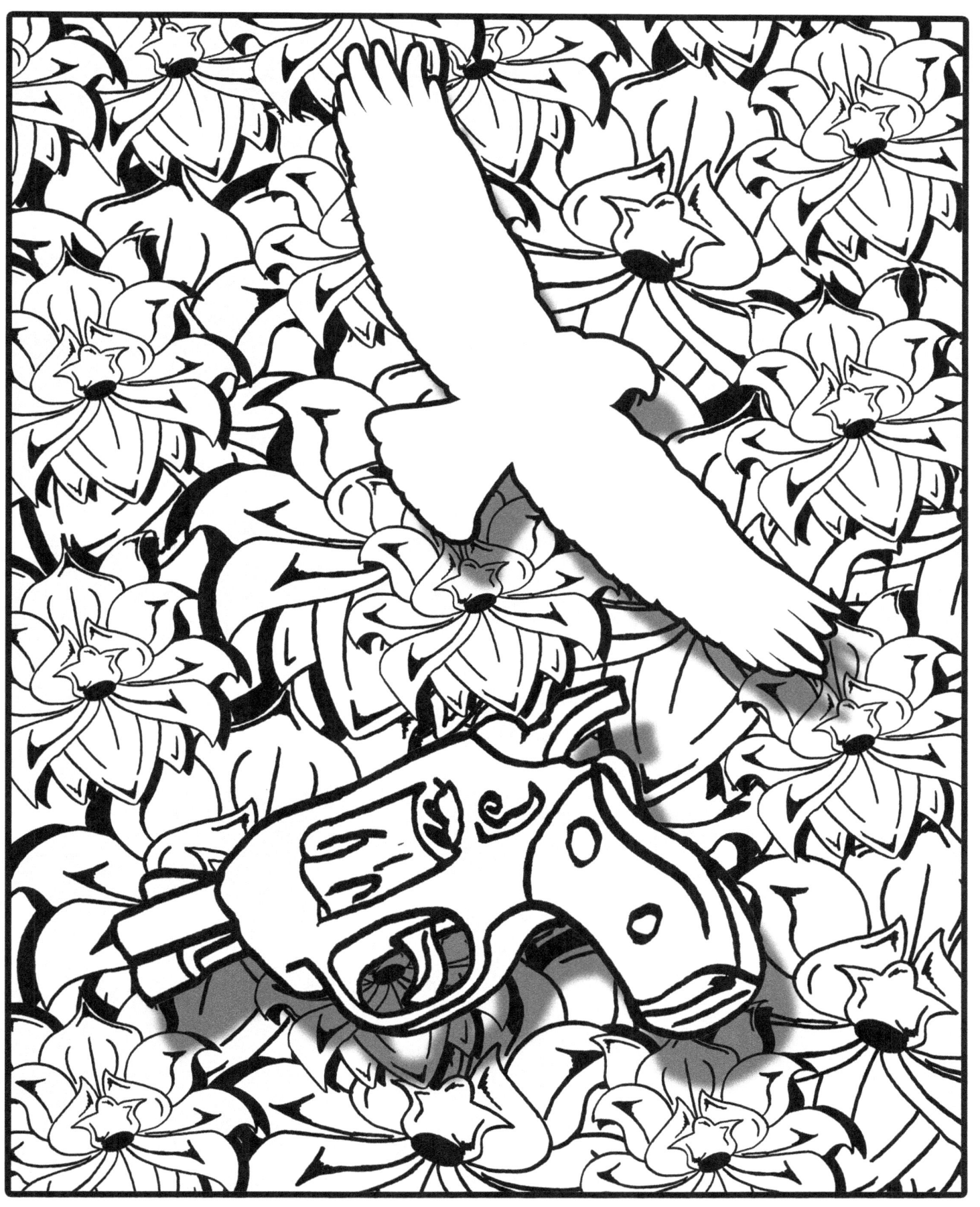

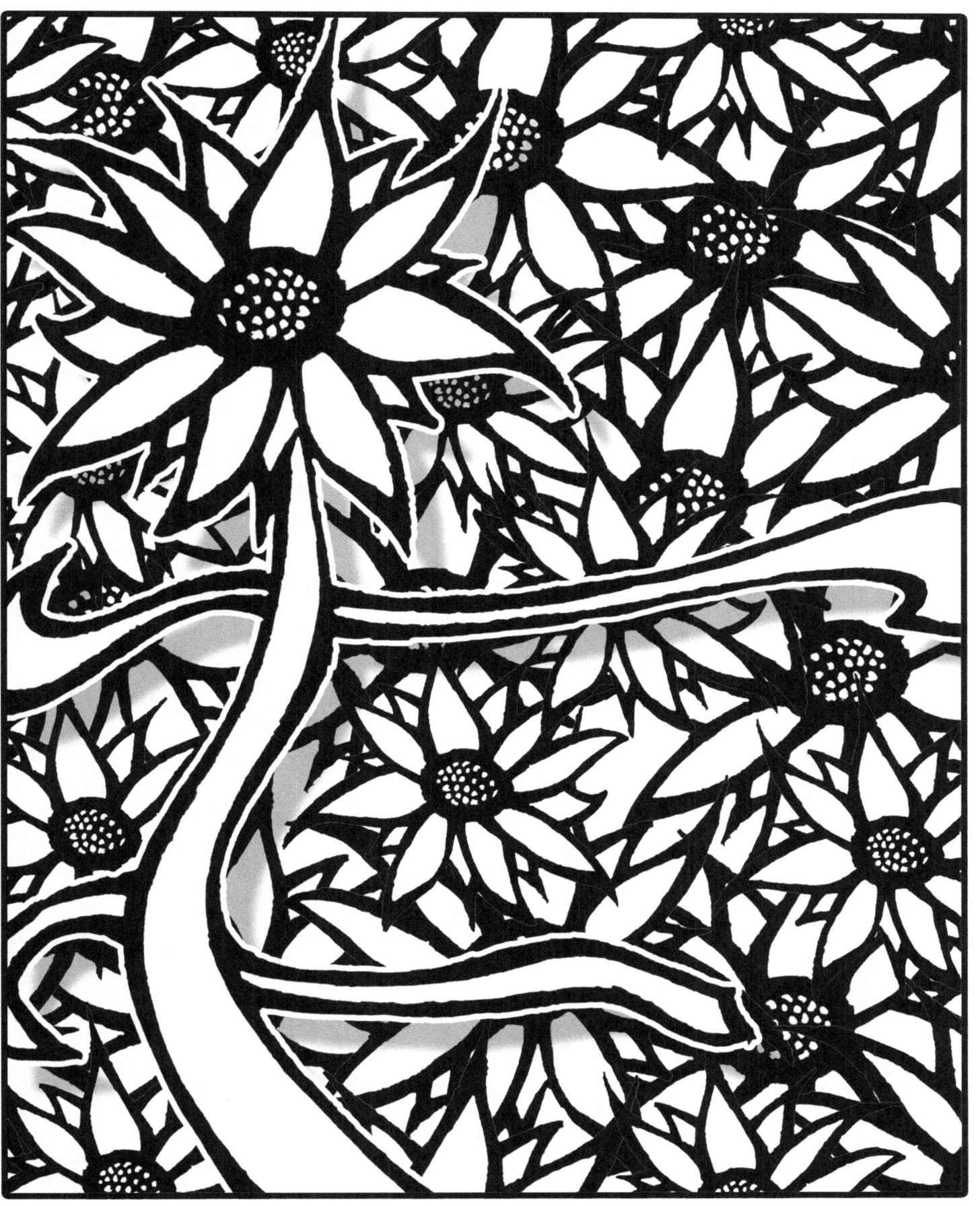

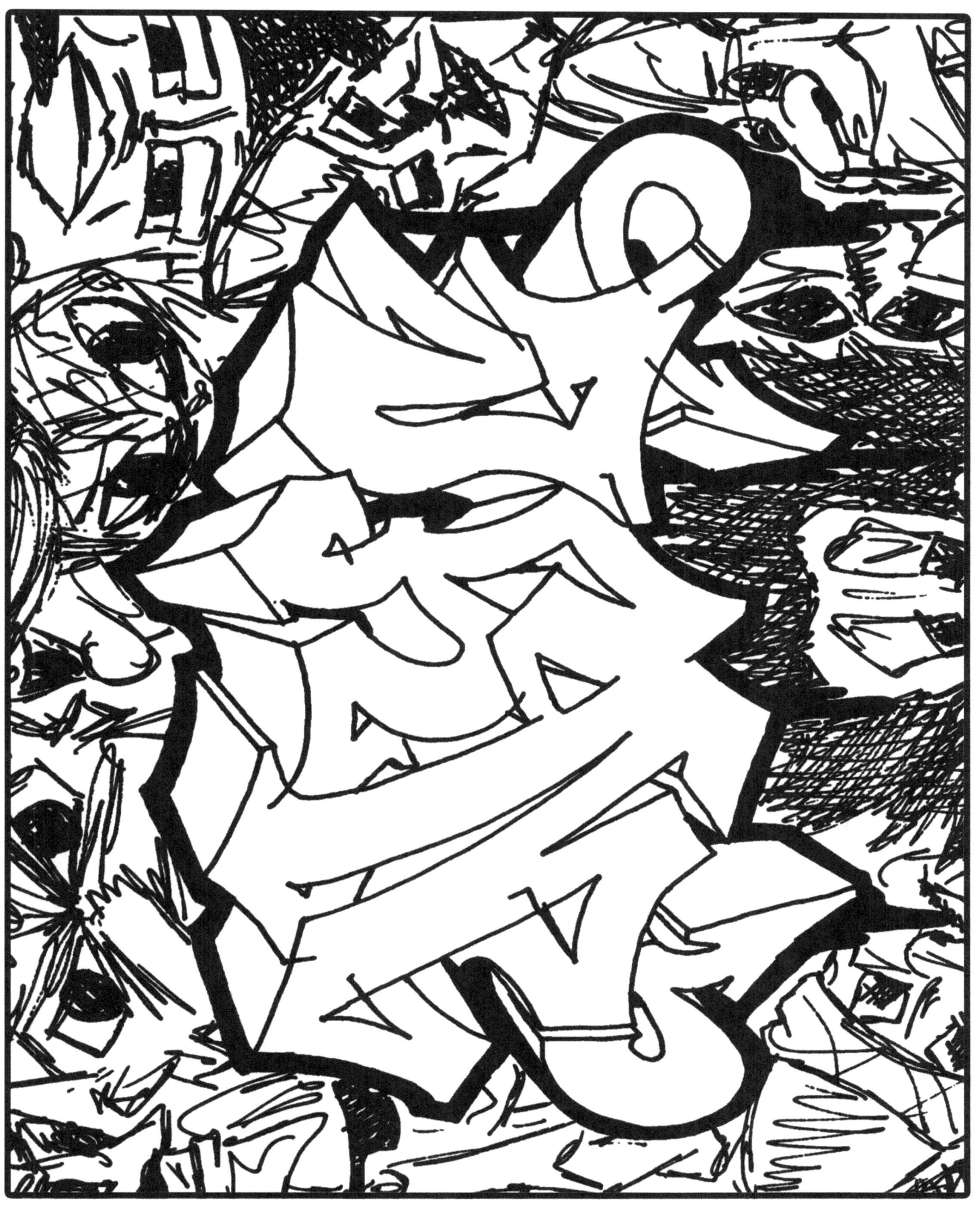

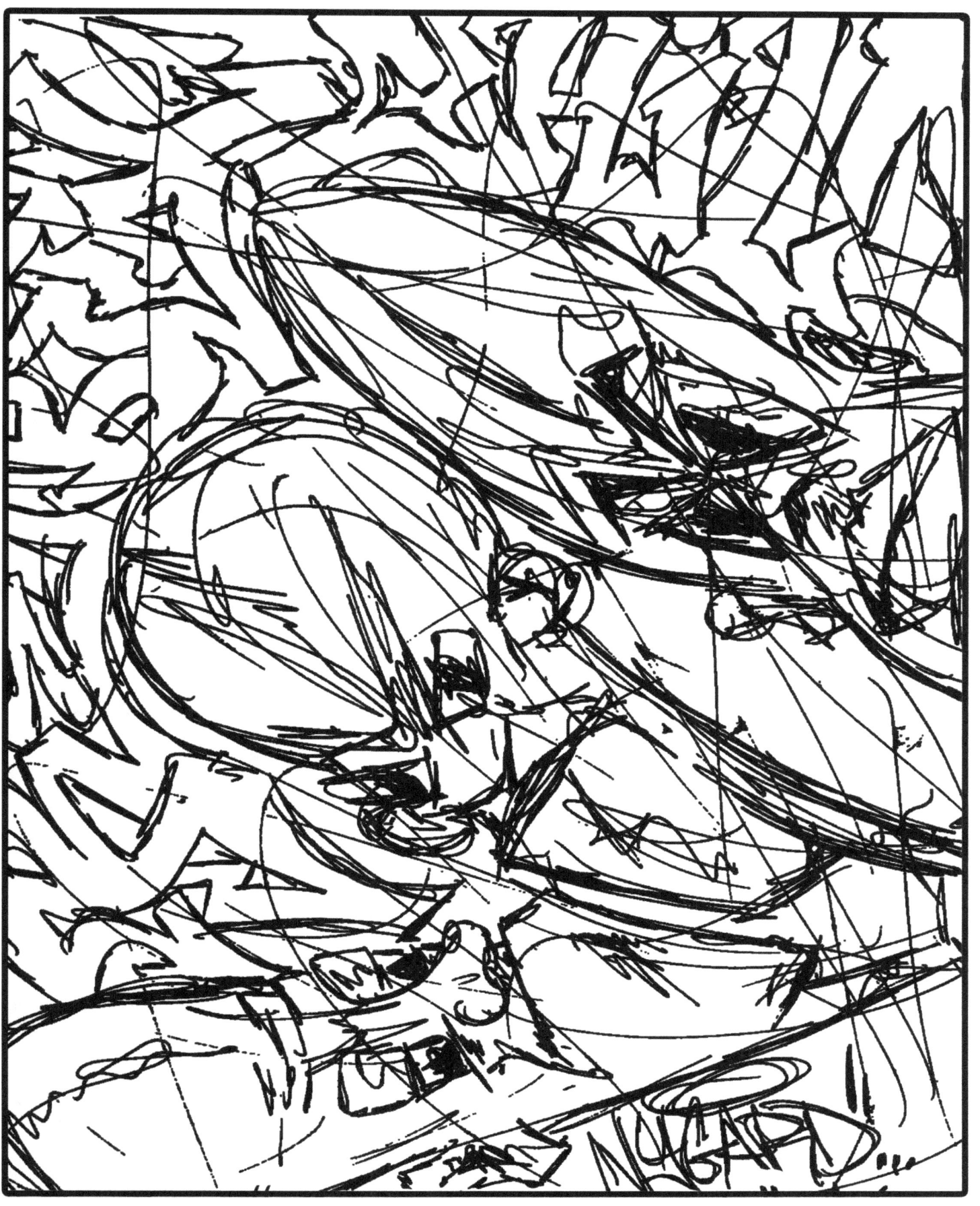

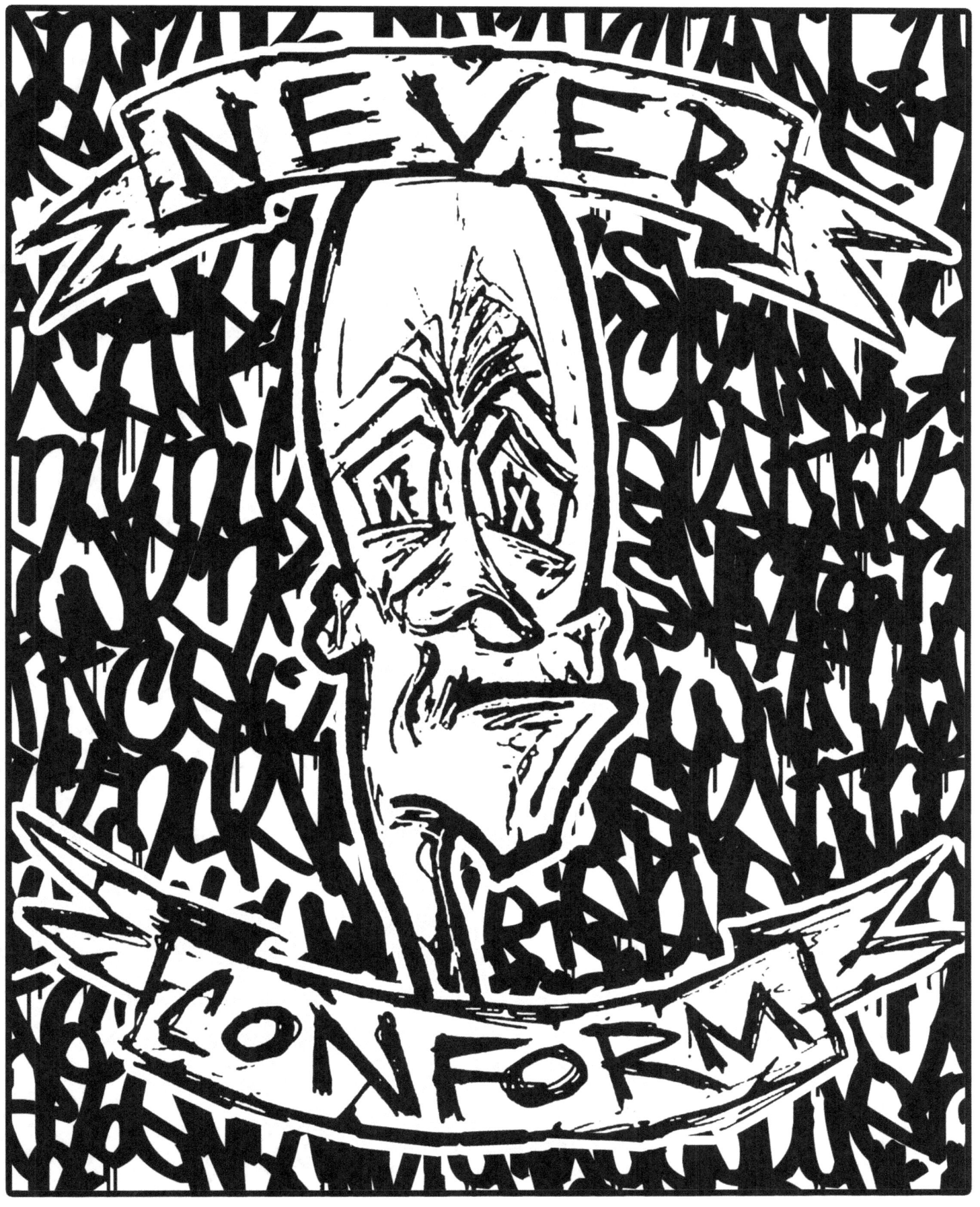